LARRY BARKDULL

Pillars of Zion Series Titles

Introduction: *Portrait of a Zion Person*

Book 1: *Zion—Our Origin and Our Destiny*

Book 2: *The First Pillar of Zion—The New and Everlasting Covenant*

Book 3: *The Second Pillar of Zion—The Oath and Covenant of the Priesthood*

Book 4: *The Third Pillar of Zion—The Law of Consecration*

Book 5: *The Pure in Heart*

Book 6: *No Poor among Them*

Pillars of Zion Publishing
Orem, Utah

Copyright and Permission

Copyright © 2009, 2013 Barkdull Marketing, Inc

Publishing Imprint: Pillars of Zion Publishing, a division of Barkdull Marketing, Inc. Licensed for publication and distributed by BestBooks Publishing and Distribution, Spanish Fork, Utah. Phone: 801.815.5349.

All Rights Reserved. No part of this book may be reproduced in any format or in any medium without the written permision from the publisher, BestBooks Publishing and Distribution.

Contact

Contact us at info@pillarsofzion.com
Visit our Website at www.PillarsOfZion.com

Disclaimer

This series is heavily documented with some 5,000 references and 400 works cited. Every effort has been made to achieve accuracy. This work is not an official publication of the Church of Jesus Christ of Latter-day Saints, and the views expressed within this work are the sole responsibility of the author and do not necessarily reflect the position of The Church of Jesus Christ of Latter-day Saints or any other entity.

LICENSE USE

1) If you received the free PDF version of the introduction to t he series *Portrait of a Zion Person,* you have the right to store it on your computer. You also have the right to share the PDF with as many people as you please, provided that neither they nor you use part or all of the content to disparage The Church of Jesus Christ of Latter-day Saints in any manner. Neither you nor anyone with whom you share the PDF has the right to change the content of the PDF.

2) If you purchased the printed book or a version of the book for an electronic reader, you do not have the right to share those versions of the book.

Refer all copyright and permissions issues to the contact above.

Library of Congress Cataloging Publication Data is on file at the Library of Congress.
ISBN: 978-09824904-8-8

Dedication
To Elizabeth Barkdull
Ron and Bonnie McMillan
David and Lorelea Anderson
Paul and Sharon Meyers

Acknowledgments
My wife, Elizabeth, and I would like to acknowledge a number of people, who, in one way or another, lent their support for the creation of this project.

>Lawrence and Georgia Shaw
>Lance and Jozet Richardson
>Blaine and Kathy Yorgason
>Scot and Maurine Proctor
>Clay Gorton
>Ted Gibbons
>Grover Cardon
>Gary and Bonnie Leavitt
>Bud and Barbara Poduska
>Dee Jay Bawden
>Steve Glenn
>Gavon and Tanya Barkdull

Production Staff
Thanks to Eschler Editing for editorial and design work.

>Editors—Jay A. Parry and Michele Preisendorf
>Graphic Artist—Douglass Cole
>Typesetter—Sean Graham

Note about The Three Pillars of Zion
The complete Zion series contains seven books. The full bibliography, and index are included in each of the books for ease of referencing and navigation. Each volume includes its own table of contents except for the Introduction book, *Portrait of a Zion Person*, includes the table of contents for each volume in order to introduce the entire series.

Table of Contents

Introduction to the Pillars of Zion Series
Portrait of a Zion Person

Portrait of a Zion Person	1
Living in the Highest Priesthood Society	3
Gathering Around Zion Principles for an Exalted Purpose	4
Embracing Beauty	5
Becoming Unified—"Of One Heart and One Mind"	6
Striving for Equality—"No Poor among Them"	7
Becoming Selfless and Giving Christian Service	8
Exhibiting the Pure Love of Christ	9
Experiencing True Happiness, Joy, and the Fullness of Life	12
Becoming Holy	14
Achieving the State of Blessedness	16
Sustaining Leaders	18
Believing Christ by Receiving Baptism and the Holy Ghost	18
Bearing Testimony	19
Becoming Poor in Spirit	19
Mourning Righteously	20
Becoming Meek	21
Hungering and Thirsting after [for] Righteousness	22
Becoming Merciful	24
Becoming Pure in Heart	25
Becoming A Maker of Peace	26
Being Willing to Suffer Persecution for the Cause of Christ	27
Experiencing True Safety and Security	29
Obtaining an Abundance in All Things	30
Embracing the Law of Consecration	33
Agency	35
Stewardship	36
Accountability	37
Labor	37
Enjoying God's Presence	39
Conclusion	41
Bibliography	45
Index and Concordance	55
About the Author	79

Book 1
Zion—Our Origin and Our Destiny

Introduction 1

    Parallels between the 3 Nephi Saints and the Latter-day Saints   1
    An Important Key to Establishing Zion   2
    Enoch's Dispensation Is a Pattern   3
    The Three Pillars of Zion   3

Section 1
Zion—What Do We Know of It? 5

    Zion Is Our Ideal   6
    The Celestial Order   7
    Zion and Babylon—Exact Opposites   7
    Becoming a Zion Person   8

Section 2
Overview of Zion Peoples 9

    Fall from Zion   9
    The Way Back to Zion Revealed   10
    Zion—A New Way of Life   12
    Surety of a Better World   12
    Adam's Zion   13
    Enos's Zion   13
    Enoch's Zion   13
    Methuselah and Noah's Zion   14
    Melchizedek's Zion   15
    Abraham's Zion   16
    Moses' Attempt at Zion   18
    Alma the Elder's Zion   19
    King Benjamin's Zion   20
    Alma the Younger's Zion   26
    The Apostles' Zion   28
    The Nephites' Zion   28
    Joseph Smith's Zion   31
    Latter-day Zion   36
    Summary and Conclusion   37

Section 3
We Were Prepared to Become
Latter-day Zion People... 39

    Divine Appointment   40
    Special Spirits of the Royal Generation   42
    Perspective on the Cosmic War   43
    Preparation in the "First Place"   44
    Summary and Conclusion   46

Section 4
Babylon the Great.. 49

    Anti-Christ Philosophy   50
    Cain   51
    Nimrod   52
    Sodom and Gomorrah   55
    Descriptions of Babylon   57
    Babylon As a Religion   60
    The "Great Church" of the Devil   61
    Babylon As a Temple   63
    Nephi's Description of Babylon   64
    Spiritual Babylon   74
    Competition   77
    Hypocrites   80
    False Philosophies   81
    Popularity   84
    Latter-day Babylon—Prophetic Description of Our Time   84
    Babylon Today Compared to the Days of Noah   86
    Paul's Prophecy   88
    Inverting the Truth   89
    Moroni's Prophecy   90
    The Fall of Babylon   92
    Samuel the Lamanite's Parallel Denunciation of Babylon   95
    Go Ye Out from Babylon   99
    Summary and Conclusion   100
    Postlude   103

Bibliography... 105

Index and Concordance 115

Book 2
The First Pillar of Zion—The New and Everlasting Covenant

Introduction 1

Section 1
Preface to the New and Everlasting Covenant 3

The Plan of Happiness	4
The Covenant of the Gods	4
Happiness Encompasses All That Is Good	5
Balancing Justice and Mercy	6
Placed beyond Our Enemies	6
How Mercy Appeases Justice	7
Experiencing Contrasts Leads to Happiness	7
Overview of the New and Everlasting Covenant	9
The Covenant of Justice	10
Who Are the Just, and How Are They Justified?	10
Justification and Agency	12
Celestial Law	13
Preserved, Perfected, and Sanctified by the Laws of God	15
Blessed As If We Understood	15
The Covenant of Mercy	16
Mercy and Grace	17
Justification	17
Purification	18
Sanctification	20
Our Responsibility	20
The Crucible—The Baptism of Fire	21
Purified and Sanctified to Make an Offering	22
Oneness or Unification	23
Oneness and the Law of Restoration	25
Restoration and Resurrection	25
Hundredfold Restoration	27
Oneness and Deliverance	27
Summary and Conclusion	28

Section 2
The New and Everlasting Covenant
The First Pillar of Zion 31

The Structure of the Covenant	32
The New and Everlasting Covenant As an Agreement	33

1. Introduction	33
2. The Covenant of Justice	34
3. The Covenant of Mercy	35
4. The Covenant of Baptism	36
Agreement to Renew and Abide in the Covenant of Baptism	37
Agreement to Live the Law of the Sabbath Day	38
5. Agreement to Receive the Covenant of the Priesthood	40
Worthy Men Agree to Be Ordained	40
Ordained Men Agree to Magnify Their Calling	42
Ordained Men Agree to Continued Faithfulness	43
6. Abide in the Covenant to the End	44
Blessings for Enduring to the End	44
The Father's Guarantee	45
Effective Signatures	45

Section 3
Abide in the Covenant 47

The Leavening Power of the Doctrine of the Covenant	48
The Covenant Separates Us from Babylon, or the World	49
Zion People Are Distinguished by Observing the Sabbath Day	50
Power in the Covenant	51
Other Powers Manifested in the Covenant	53
Safety in the Covenant	54
Safety through Consecration in the Covenant	55
The Great Discovery	57
Examples of Safety in the Covenant	57
Progressing in the Covenant	60
Discovering the Relationship through Progression	61
Order in the Covenant	62
Order and Ordinances	63
Order and Consecration	64
Abide in the Covenant	64
Abiding in the Covenant Summons Divine Love	66
Abiding in the Covenant through the Sacrament	67
Summary and Conclusion	67

Section 4
The New and Everlasting Covenant—The Holy Marriage 71

Born to Marry	72
The Parents' Responsibility and the Bride's Choice	73
Requirements to Legalize the Covenant	74

Initiating the Marriage Proposal	74
Entering into the Covenant	75
Bought with a Price	76
The Marriage Contract	77
The Gift of Value	79
The Pledge	80
The Cup to Seal the Covenant	81
The Covenantal Feast	82
The Father's Announcement	82
The Bride's Veil	83
The Friend of the Bridegroom	84
Preparing for Each Other	85
The Serious Nature of Preparing	87
The Bride's Final Preparations	89
Invitation to the Wedding	91
The Wedding Processional	92
Claiming the Bride	93
The Wedding	94
The Bridegroom's Plea	97
Postlude	98

Bibliography 101

Index and Concordance 111

Book 3
The Second Pillar of Zion—
The Oath and Covenant of the Priesthood

Introduction 1

Section 1
The Holy Priesthood after the
Order of the Son of God 3

The Doctrines of the Priesthood As They Apply to Men and Women	4
Melchizedek, the Title and the Man	4
King Benjamin, a Type of Melchizedek	7
The Restoration of the Priesthood	12
Elijah Restores the Sealing Keys of the Patriarchal Order of the Priesthood	12
Elijah Restores the Fulness of the Priesthood	13
Moses Restores Priesthood Keys of Family Gathering	14

Elias Restores Priesthood Keys	14
The Joint Missions of Elias and Elijah	15
Building One Priesthood Power upon Another	16
Rescuing This Generation	17
Eternal Principle of Power	17
Premortal Qualification for the Priesthood	18
The Obligation of Zion Priesthood Holders	19
Our Priesthood Work Then and Now	20
The Covenant of the Priesthood	21
The Lesser and Greater Portions	22
The Patriarchal Order	22
Differing Purposes and Powers	23
Grand Purposes of the Priesthood	24
Priesthood Blessings	24
The Blessings of Adam	25
The Blessings of Abraham	26
Abraham's Qualifications and Desire	28
Blessings of the Priesthood	29
The Prize Is Worth the Price	30
The Authority and Keys of the Priesthood	31
Doctrine of the Priesthood	33
"As My Father Hath Sent Me, Even So Send I You"	35
Summary and Conclusion	35

Section 2
The Oath and Covenant of the Priesthood
Our Agreements 39

If We Are Faithful . . .	41
If We Magnify Our *Calling* . . .	43
Magnifying the *Calling* and *Callings*	44
Three Ways to Magnify Our Calling	46
Obtaining Gospel Knowledge	46
Personal Righteousness	47
Dedicated Service	51
Grace *to* Grace by Grace *for* Grace	52
If Any of You Lack	54
Magnifying Our Priesthood Calling by Bearing Testimony	55
The Ultimate Magnification of Our *Calling*	57
The Three Stages of the Priesthood Covenant	58
Summary and Conclusion	59

Section 3
The Oath and Covenant of the Priesthood
The Father's Oath, Instructions, and Promises 63

The Father's Two Oaths Guaranteeing Us the Blessings of Abraham	64
Sanctification by the Spirit unto the Renewing of Our Bodies	66
The Progression of the Renewing of Our Bodies	67
Power Given to the Renewed and Sanctified	69
Blessings Given to the Renewed and Sanctified	70
"I Sanctify Myself, That They Also Might Be Sanctified"	74
The Sons of Moses and of Aaron	76
The Seed of Abraham	78
The Church and Kingdom of God	79
The Elect of God	79
Calling and Election Made Sure	81
Receiving Christ and the Father	85
"All That My Father Hath"	88
Ministering and Protection of Angels	90
The Father's Instructions: *Be Careful and Be Diligent*	94
"And the Father Teacheth Him of the Covenant"	95
The Promise of Eternal Life	98
Penalties for Neglecting or Rejecting the Covenant of the Priesthood	102
Summary and Conclusion	103

Section 4
The Constitution of the Priesthood
Why Many Are Called but Not Chosen 107

Two Groups	108
A Satanic Strategy	109
A Test of Loyalties	109
Restoration of the Constitution of the Priesthood	110
The Marriage of the King's Son	111
"Many Will Say to Me in That Day"	113
Called and Chosen for Eternal Life	114
Abiding Zion's Celestial Law in Babylon's Telestial Setting	116
The End Purpose of Our Calling	117
Distinctions between Those Who Are Called and Those Who Are Chosen	118
Building a Sure House	119
Mortal Tests That Challenge Our Calling	120
The Daunting Test of Riches	122
Safety and Perfection in Consecration	123
The Sacrifice of All Things—A "Hard Thing"	123

Safety in the "Royal Law"	124
The Dangers of Rationalization and Postponement	125
The Law of Restitution—An *Hundredfold* Reward	126
Babylon among Us	127
Walking in Darkness at Noon-day	130
The Test of Praise	131
"Rights of the Priesthood"	134
"Inseparably Connected"—Righteousness and Priesthood Power	135
Connecting to the True Vine	135
Amen to the Priesthood	137
Summary and Conclusion	139

Section 5
The Constitution of the Priesthood
Instructing the Chosen Few 143

Stages of Progression within the Covenant	144
No Power or Influence Can or Ought to Be Maintained by Virtue of the Priesthood	145
Zion's Approach to Agency	146
Persuasion versus Babylon's Counterparts	147
Zion's Patient Persuasion	147
Patience and Long-suffering	147
Patience	148
Long-suffering	150
Gentleness and Meekness	151
Feigned and Unfeigned Love	153
What Is "True Love"?	155
To Love First	156
Love Perfected	157
No Fear in Love	158
Love—The Greatest Power	158
Kindness	159
Pure Knowledge versus False Knowledge	159
Zion's Approach to "Pure Knowledge"	164
Wisdom and Pure Knowledge	167
Reproving the Lord's Way	168
Reproving with Love	169
Cords of Death and Bonds of Love	170
Charity toward All Men and the Household of God	171
Let Virtue Garnish Thy Thoughts Unceasingly	172
Garnishing Our Thoughts with Virtue	173
Summary and Conclusion	173

Section 6
The Constitution of the Priesthood
The Rewards for the Chosen Few 175

    The Rewards   175
    "Then Shall Thy Confidence Wax Strong in the Presence of God"   176
    Now Is the Time   177
    A Change of Paradigm   178
    Turning the *Key*   179
    Obtaining, at Last, a Perfect Knowledge of the Savior   180
    Receiving the Greatest Comfort   181
    Regaining the Presence of God—The End Purpose of the Priesthood   182
    The Revealed Process for Standing in the Presence of God   182
    The Priesthood Is the Power to Stand in God's Presence   183
    "The Doctrine of the Priesthood Shall Distil upon Thy Soul"   184
    The Rights and the Doctrine of the Priesthood   186
    The Doctrine of the Priesthood and the Law of Asking   187
    Lesser and Greater Portions of the Doctrine of the Priesthood   189
    The Necessity and Power of Priesthood Ordinances   189
    The Doctrine of the Priesthood and Revelatory "Keys"   191
    "The Holy Ghost Shall Be Thy Constant Companion"   193
    The Holy Spirit of Promise   194
    Scepters and Dominions—The Holy Interview   194
    Priests and Kings, Priestesses and Queens   197
    Becoming Members of the Church of the Firstborn   200
    Angelic Ministers from the Church of the Firstborn   202
    The Order of the Son of God   204
    The Order of the Son of God and Marriage   206
    The Fulness of the Priesthood   208
    Power in the Priesthood   208
    "Without Compulsory Means It Shall Flow unto Thee Forever"   210
    Summary and Conclusion   211
    Postlude   214

Bibliography 215

Index and Concordance 225

Book 4
The Third Pillar of Zion—The Law of Consecration

Introduction 1

Section 1
What Is the Law of Consecration? 3

Consecration—the Principle of Exaltation	3
The Condition of Babylon	5
The Greatest Desire	6
Definition of Consecration	6
The Law We Must Live to Achieve the Celestial Kingdom	8
Consecrating the Good and the Bad	8
Premise of Consecration	9
Consecration Is Nonnegotiable	10
Restoration of the Law of Consecration	10
Consecrating Tithes and Offerings	12
Modern Applications of Consecration	13
Learning to Better Live the Law of Consecration	14
Sanctified by Consecration: The Law of the Celestial Kingdom	14
Familiarity	15
Ultimate Consecration—To Sacrifice a Prepared and Purified Heart	16
Live Consecration or Lose Eternal Life	17
Laying Everything on the Altar	17
Consecration and the Atonement	18
Consecration—A Temporal Law with Spiritual Implications	20
Consecration—A Law That Makes Us Independent from the World	21
Consecration—An Order That Orders Our Lives	25
What Consecration Is Not	27
Temporal and Spiritual Salvation	28
Summary and Conclusion	29

Section 2
Consecration Results in Equality and Unity 33

Equality—"In Mine Own Way"	33
Equality and the Law of Prosperity	34
New Math	36
Esteeming All Flesh in One	36
Seven Points of Equality	37
Taking Equal Responsibility for the Cause of Zion	39

Unity	40
The Unifying Power of the At-one-ment	41
Oneness and Synergy	43
Antagonism—The Opposite of Synergy	44
Unity and Prayer	45
How We Achieve Unity	46
The End Result of Unity	47
All Things Common among Them	47
Consecration and the Law of Offense	48
Law of Common Consent	49
Connecting Consecration with the Law of the Gospel and the Law of Sacrifice	50
Love Leads Us to Eternal Life	51
Is Baptism Sufficient for Exaltation?	52
Two Purposes of the Law of the Gospel	52
No Other Way	53
The Interwoven Covenants	54
The Law of Sacrifice	55
Sacrifice and love	55
Sacrifice—Our Contribution to Our Salvation	56
Summary and Conclusion	58

Section 3
The Guiding Principles of Consecration 61

Guiding Principles of Consecration	62
Agency	62
Agency and Truth	62
Agency—A Gift Assured and Protected by the Savior	63
The Body—The Vehicle for Moral Agency	63
Our Eternal Destiny Lies within Our Body	64
Agency and Agents	65
Agency and Self-reliance	66
The Power of Choice	67
Stewardship	68
The Riches of the Earth Are the Lord's	68
God Becomes Our Paymaster	70
Never Turn Back	71
The Law of Stewardship and the Oath and Covenant of the Priesthood	72
Stewardship and Equality	73
Stewardships in the Scriptures	74
Understanding the Order of the Law of Stewardship	75
Spiritual Gifts Are Stewardships to Bless Others	76
Profitable and Unprofitable Servants	78

Stewardships Prepare Us for Eternal Life	79
Accountability	80
Accounting in Time and Eternity	80
Accountability and Agency	81
Labor	82
Idleness Condemned	83
The Idle Poor	83
The Idle Rich	85
The Virtue of Labor	86
Labor for What?	86
Augmenting the Effect of Labor	88
Labor and Judgment	89
Summary and Conclusion	90

Section 4
The Ultimate Test: God or Mammon 93

The Test of Riches	94
Only the Pure in Heart Can Pass This Test	95
The Lord's Willingness to Be Tested	96
Consecration Is All about Love	97
A Change of Orders	98
Love of Money Is the Root of *All* Evil	99
Covetousness—The Last Law	100
The Higher and Lower Laws of Prosperity	101
The More Weighty Matters	102
Trying to Mix Mammon and Zion	102
Warnings against Compromise	105
Making Mammon Holy	106
Mormon's View of the Last Days	107
The First Commandments of This Dispensation	107
No Security in Mammon	109
Slippery Treasures	110
Lazarus and the Rich Man	111
Nothing Compares to the Danger	113
Lessons in the Scriptures Concerning Wealth	115
Scriptural Description of the Last Days	116
Scriptures about Idolatry and Wealth	117
Scriptures about Seeking Wealth and Forgetting God	117
Scriptures about Mammon, Inequality, and Divisiveness	118
Scriptural Evidence That the Lord Despises the Selfish Rich	120
Persecuting the Poor	121
Wo unto the Rich Who Despise the Poor	122

They Rob the Poor	123
Building Sanctuaries	123
Wealth-Seeking—The Sin That Hinders and Destroys the Church	124
The Ugliness of Inequality Contrasted with the Beautiful Work of Angels	125
Withholding from and Judging the Poor Harshly	126
The Evil of the Age: Life for Money	126
A Curse on the Daughters of Zion	128
Blessings for Those Who Rescue the Poor	129
The Poor of the Lord's People Shall Trust in Zion	130
Consequences of Seeking Wealth and Persecuting the Poor	131
Loss of the Providences of Heaven	132
Loss of Priesthood Power and Exaltation	132
Loss of the Spirit	133
Loss of Revelation	133
Loss of Happy Family Life and Spiritual Commitment	133
Loss of the Lord's Help	134
Loss of True Worship	134
Failure in Our Mission	135
Loss of Peace	135
Loss of National Security	138
Who Shall Enter?	138
What Doth It Profit?	139
The Voice of Seven Thunders	141
Choosing God over Mammon	141
Obtaining a Hope in Christ	142
Freely Ye Have Received, Freely Give	144
Feeding the Lord's Lambs	145
Choosing God's Marvelous Work over Babylon's Charms	146
Invoking the Law of Asking to Receive	146
Summary and Conclusion	147

Section 5
The Royal Law 155

The Royal Law Explains the Principles of Consecration	156
Doctrine and Covenants 42—The Cornerstones of the Law of Consecration	157
Mutual Assistance	158
Faith and the Proper Use of the Priesthood	158
Announcing the Kingdom of Heaven through Administrations	160
Consecrating a Sickness and a Life to the Lord	160
Administration and Forgiveness of Sins	162
Consecration Requires Faith	162
Reciprocal Love	163

Charity—The Pure Love of Christ	165
Charity Strengthened by Faith and Hope	166
Charity Transforms the Heart	167
Charity Defines Discipleship	168
Keeping and Feeding—The Two Tests of Charity	169
Charity—The Lifeblood of Zion	170
Charity Is Defined by Service	171
Charitable Service Saves and Exalts	174
Moroni's Prayer for Latter-day Charity	174
Charitable Service Protects the Giver	175
Charitable Service Prospers the Giver	176
Patience and Charity	178
Charity and Virtue—Essential Elements of Priesthood Power	178
Charity Draws the Lord Near	179
Charity Is an Absolute	181
Charity Is a Gift—The Greatest Gift	181
Summary and Conclusion	182
Postlude	185

Bibliography 187

Index and Concordance 197

Book 5
The Pure in Heart

Introduction 1

Section 1
Come to Zion: The Universal Journey to the Land of Promise 7

Zion Is Our Heritage	8
The Fall	11
The Wilderness of Sin	12
The Awakening	14
The Cry for Help	15
The Lord's Wilderness	17
Experiencing Opposites	18
Strangers and Pilgrims	19
Separation from Babylon	19
Fleeing for Safety	21

The Crucible	23
The Tragedy of Murmuring	26
Finding Joy in the Journey	27
Conditions of the Lord's Wilderness	30
Living by Manna	31
Hard Work	32
Traveling by Revelation	33
Journeying According to the Lord's Will	35
Angels Attend Us	35
Safety and Security	37
Deliverance Experiences	38
The Fourth Watch	39
Lessons to Be Learned in the Lord's Wilderness	41
Preparation to Live the Higher Law	41
Putting Off the Natural Man	42
Learning the Formula of Obedience	45
Learning to Trust God: The Universal Lesson	47
Bountiful—A Reprieve	52
Confronting Satan	54
The Abrahamic Test	56
Taking upon Us the Name of Jesus Christ	59
Taking upon Us the Name of Christ through Baptism and the Sacrament	60
Common Ways of Taking upon Ourselves the Name of Christ	61
Born of God—The Mystery of Spiritual Rebirth	61
Fully Taking upon Us the Name of Jesus Christ	62
The Temple and the Name of Christ	64
The Name of Christ and Coronation	65
Coming to Christ	66
Deliverance	68
Giving Ourselves Free	70
Restoration and Exaltation	72
Sent Back as an Emissary of Zion	74
Summary and Conclusion	75

Section 2
The Pure in Heart 77

Blessings for the Pure in Heart	78
Commanded to Seek the Lord's Face	78
Purification	79
Sanctification	80
Who May Seek the Lord's Face?	80
How Do We Come into the Presence of the Lord?	81
Knowing and Living the Correct Process	82
Knowing and Living the Higher Law and Its Principles of Progression	82

Receiving Power from on High	83
Receiving More Doctrine	83
Receiving More Doctrine by Choice	84
Receiving More Doctrine by Desire	85
Receiving More Doctrine by Faith	85
Receiving More Doctrine by Persistence and Improvement	85
Receiving More Doctrine by Service	86
Receiving More Doctrine by Seeking	86
Receiving More Doctrine by Treasuring Up	86
The Significance of the Temple Recommend	87
By What Power Might We Seek the Lord's Face?	87
Holiness to the Lord	90
A New Commitment	91
"It Is High Time to Establish Zion"	93
Priesthood Holders Must Set the Example	95
A Few Could Form the Foundation of Zion	96
According to Revelation	98
Our Duty to Individually Become Zion	100
3 Nephi—Latter-day Guide to Establishing Zion	101
"Which We Might Have Received in One Year"	105
The Pure in Heart *Shall* See God	109
The Father's Testimony	110
The Savior's Testimony	110
Coming Forth to See and Know	111
Rejoicing, Worshipping, and Bearing Testimony	112
Receiving an Endowment of Knowledge	112
Healing	113
The Savior's Prayer for Us and Our Prayer to Him	114
Encircled About by Angels	116
Partaking of the Lord's Supper in His Presence	117
Receiving a Greater Endowment of the Holy Ghost	117
The Hundredfold Law	118
Revelations, Prophecies, and Explanations	118
Greater Commandments	119
The Greater Commandment to Pray Always	120
The Greater Commandment to Have All Things in Common	122
The Greater Commandment to Be "Even As the Lord Is"	123
Receiving a Special Gift	125
Beautiful Zion	127
Blessings for the Beautiful Ones	130
Summary and Conclusion—The Three Pillars of Zion	132

Bibliography 139

Index and Concordance 149

Book 6
No Poor among Them

Introduction
The Dream of a Better World 1

    Giving Opens the Doors to Blessings   2
    Laying the Foundation   3
    Lessons from the Good Samaritan   5

Chapter 1
The Ultimate Test—God or Mammon 7

    The Test of Riches   8
    Only the Pure in Heart Can Pass This Test   9
    The Lord's Willingness to Be Tested   10
    Consecration Is All about Love   11
    A Coming Change of Orders   12
    Conclusion   12

Chapter 2
Thou Shalt Not Covet—The Last Law 15

    Covetousness—The Last Law   16
    The Higher and Lower Laws of Prosperity   17
    The More Weighty Matters   18
    Trying to Mix Mammon and Zion   19
    Warnings Against Compromise   21
    Making Mammon Holy   21
    Mormon's View of the Last Days   22

Chapter 3
The First Commandments of This Dispensation 25

    No Security in Mammon   26
    Slippery Treasures   27
    Lazarus and the Rich Man   29
    Nothing Compares to the Danger   30
    Take Heed and Beware of Covetousness   31

Chapter 4
Lessons in the Scriptures Concerning Wealth   33

    Scriptural Description of the Last Days   35
    Scriptures about Idolatry and Wealth   35

Scriptures about Seeking Wealth and Forgetting God ... 36
Scriptures about Mammon, Inequality, and Divisiveness ... 37
Scriptural Evidence That the Lord Despises the Selfish Rich ... 38

Chapter 5
Persecuting the Poor ... 41

Wo unto the Rich Who Despise the Poor ... 42
They Rob the Poor ... 42
Building Personal Sanctuaries ... 43
Wealth-Seeking—The Sin That Hinders and Destroys the Church ... 44
The Ugliness of Inequality Contrasted with the Beautiful Work of Angels ... 45
Withholding from and Judging the Poor Harshly ... 46
The Evil of the Age: Life for Money ... 47
A Curse on the Daughters of Zion ... 48
Blessings for Those Who Rescue the Poor ... 49
The Poor of the Lord's People Shall Trust in Zion ... 52

Chapter 6
Consequences of Seeking Wealth and Persecuting the Poor ... 55

Loss of the Providences of Heaven ... 56
Loss of Priesthood Power and Exaltation ... 56
Loss of the Spirit ... 56
Loss of Revelation ... 56
Loss of Happy Family Life and Spiritual Commitment ... 57
Loss of the Lord's Help ... 58
Loss of True Worship ... 58
Failure in Our Mission ... 58
Loss of Peace ... 59
Loss of National Security ... 61

Chapter 7
Who Shall Enter? ... 63

What Doth It Profit? ... 64
The Voice of Seven Thunders ... 65
Choosing God over Mammon ... 66
Obtaining a Hope in Christ ... 67
Freely Ye Have Received, Freely Give ... 68
Feeding the Lord's Lambs ... 68
Choosing God's Marvelous Work over Babylon's Charms ... 69
Invoking the Law of Asking to Receive ... 70
Conclusion ... 71

Chapter 8
Becoming the Pure in Heart 75

Burning Out Impurities — 76
Persecution of the poor — 77
Inequality — 77
Charitable Service Propels Zion — 79
Grace *to* Grace by Grace *for* Grace — 80
Lacking for Nothing — 80
If Any of You Lack — 82

Chapter 9
Charity—The Lifeblood of Zion 85

Charity Defines Discipleship — 86
Keeping and Feeding—The Two Tests of Charity — 86
Charity—The Lifeblood of Zion — 87
Charity Is Defined by Service — 87
Charitable Service Saves and Exalts — 88
Charitable Service Protects the Giver — 88
Charitable Service Prospers the Giver — 89
Charity Is an Absolute — 90
Charity Is a Gift—The Greatest Gift — 90

Chapter 10
Without Charity We Are Nothing 93

Charity—The Pure Love of Christ — 94
Charity Emerges from Faith and Hope — 95
Charity Transforms the Heart — 96
Charity Promotes Equality, Unity and an Abundant Life — 97
Charitable Service Saves and Exalts — 99
Moroni's Prayer for Latter-day Charity — 100
Patience and Charity — 101
Charity and Virtue—Essential Elements of Priesthood Power — 101
Charity Draws the Lord Near — 102
Charity Empowers All Gospel Laws — 104

Chapter 11
The Hundredfold Law 105

The Law of Restoration — 106
Struggling with Zion and Babylon Principles — 106

New Math	107
What Doth It Profit to Cling to Our Property?	108
Safety and Perfection in Consecration	108
The Hundredfold Law	109
Freely Ye Have Received, Freely Give	110

Chapter 12
Ultimate Abundance, Safety, and Security 111

True Safety and Security	112
Obtaining an Abundance in All Things	112
Telestial and Celestial Wealth	112
Wealth-seeking is Strictly Forbidden	113
God or Mammon—The Ultimate Test	114
Abundance and Personal Righteousness	114
Exceedingly Prosperous	115
Postlude	115

Bibliography 119

Index and Concordance 129

Portrait of a Zion Person

> This book is a concise introduction to the expansive series entitled The Three Pillars of Zion. Within its pages, we will identify and provide a brief overview of several (not all) characteristics that might portray a Zion person. In the seven subsequent books, we will discuss these characteristics, along with others, as we explore in depth the unique covenants, attributes, powers, and privileges of a Zion person.

We speak of Zion, sing of Zion and long for Zion, but what do we know of it? That we must have wanted to live in the days of Zion and become Zion people is evidenced by our being born in the latter days and enjoying the blessings of Zion. We likely prepared for Zion in the premortal life, and perhaps we asked and were assigned to come at this time to help and establish Zion. With little doubt, Zion was and is our desire.

We live at a time when the three covenants or "pillars" of Zion—The new and everlasting covenant, the oath and covenant of the priesthood, and the law of consecration—have been restored to the earth.[1] Thus, we have immediate access to the blessings of Zion. What remains is our understanding these covenants and our abiding faithfully in them. That is, we must lift our sights, believe, and implement *all* the terms of the covenants in our lives. Only then can we achieve the ideal of the characteristics that describe Zion people.

When a person seeks to faithfully live *all* the terms of the three pillars of Zion, he qualifies for an unequalled harvest of blessings. If we were to attempt to describe a Zion person who abides in these covenants, we would discover that his set of characteristics would be light-years removed from the description of a person of Babylon. Among his characteristics might be the following:

Living in the highest priesthood society
Gathering around Zion principles for an exalted purpose
Embracing beauty
Becoming unified—"one heart and one mind"
Striving for equality—"no poor among them"
Becoming selfless and giving Christian service

---

1   D&C 42:67.

Exhibiting the pure love of Christ
Experiencing true happiness, joy, and fullness of life
Becoming holy
Achieving the state of *blessedness* by
- Sustaining leaders
- Believing Christ by receiving baptism and the Holy Ghost
- Bearing testimony
- Becoming poor in spirit
- Mourning righteously
- Becoming meek
- Hungering and thirsting for righteousness
- Becoming merciful
- Becoming pure in heart
- Becoming a maker of peace
- Being willing to suffer persecution for the cause of Christ

Experiencing true safety and security
Obtaining an abundance in all things
Embracing the law of consecration with its four foundational principles:
- Agency
- Stewardship
- Accountability
- Labor

Enjoying God's presence

While these qualities, characteristics, and attributes are not inclusive, they do provide a basis by which we might paint the portrait of a Zion person.

Introduction   Portrait of a Zion Person

Living in the Highest Priesthood Society

Earthly societies exist in varying levels, from telestial to celestial. President Kimball called Zion, "the highest order of priesthood society."[2] When ancient Zion people entered into the new and everlasting covenant, they, as individuals and as priesthood societies, flourished beyond imagination. The best known of these priesthood societies were the cities of Enoch, Salem, and the Nephites in their golden era.[3] The Melchizedek Priesthood, with its ordination and ordinances, has the power to prepare people for the Lord to establish Zion in individual lives, marriages, families, and in a priesthood society.[4] The fundamental priesthood society, of course, is the family; hence, the continuing admonition of the prophets is to create Zion in our homes. For example, Elder Matthew Cowley said, "In your homes where the priesthood of God exists, there is Zion."[5] Hence, Zion is family centered, just as it is in heaven.

Pure-hearted people who embrace the new and everlasting covenant (the Covenant[6]) seek to first embrace Zion principles in their individual lives; then they seek for the establishment of Zion in their marriages, families and, of course, in the Church. They become ambassadors of Zion, and they dedicate their lives to drawing people out of Babylon and into Zion. They "arise and shine forth, that [their] light may be a standard for the nations."[7] By means of the power of the priesthood and the Zion principles of righteousness, they are eventually brought back into the presence of God and obtain heaven, the celestial environment and ideal of Zion.[8]

---

2   Kimball, "And the Lord Called His People Zion," 2.
3   Moses 6:67; JST, Genesis 14:27, 32–34; 4 Nephi 1:1–18.
4   D&C 113:8; 84:19–22.
5   Cowley, *Matthew Cowley Speaks*, 30.
6   In this book, when the word *Covenant* is capitalized, it is referring to the new and everlasting covenant.
7   D&C 115:5.
8   See JST, Genesis 14:26–32.

Gathering Around Zion Principles for an Exalted Purpose

Jeremiah spoke of the Lord's intention to gather us to and make us individually Zion: "I will take you one of a city, and two of a family, and I will bring you to Zion."[9] Zion, as a priesthood society, can be subdivided into stakes[10] and wards, and further subdivided into families.[11] The purpose of gathering to Zion, or gathering around Zion principles, is always the same: "to raise up a committed society of 'pure people' who will 'serve God in righteousness' (D&C 100:13, 16)."[12] To that end, Moses restored the keys of gathering to the Prophet Joseph Smith in the Kirtland Temple, a significant principle of priesthood power that parents might ponder with regard to their family.[13]

A reason that Zion individuals gather to Zion and around Zion principles in their marriages, families, wards, and stakes is to become *one,* or unified. Jesus taught that there is inherent power in unity: "Verily, verily, I say unto you, as I said unto my disciples, where two or three are gathered together in my name, as touching one thing, behold, there will I be in the midst of them—even so am I in the midst of you."[14] Besides marriages, families, wards and stakes, Zion people gather in presidencies, home teaching, visiting teaching, in missionary companionships, or wherever two or more are gathered in the Lord's name. When we gather together "as touching one thing,"[15] we invite the Lord to join with and help us. The principle of gathering summons extraordinary power when exercised in righteousness.

---

9   Jeremiah 3:4.
10   D&C 101:21–22.
11   Cowley, *Matthew Cowley Speaks,* 30.
12   *Encyclopedia of Mormonism,* s.v. "Zion," 1624; see also D&C 43:8–11; Ephesians 4:11–13.
13   D&C 110:11.
14   D&C 6:32; see also Matthew 18:20.
15   D&C 6:32.

Embracing Beauty

Zion is the perfection of beauty.[16] This could be said of a Zion person. Besides meaning outward loveliness, the word *beauty* suggests harmony, excellence, truthfulness, originality. Beauty draws attention to something or someone's most effective features. Moreover, beauty is gratifying and defined as an outstanding or conspicuous example.[17] No wonder, then, that the Lord commands that "Zion must increase in beauty, and in holiness. . . Zion must arise and put on her beautiful garments."[18] Hugh Nibley wrote:

> The two words most commonly used to describe Zion are beauty and joy, and the same two words most often relate to heaven and paradise. Beauty comes first, for beauty is whatever gives joy. Now we approach the question of what Zion looks like: "The city of our God. . . Beautiful for situation, the joy of the whole earth, is mount Zion. . . Walk about Zion and go round about her" (Psalm 48:1–2, 11–12). "An eminently delightful place. . . " These are more than figures of speech. As President Joseph F. Smith put it, "Things upon the earth, so far as they have not been perverted by wickedness, are typical of things in heaven. Heaven was the prototype of this beautiful creation when it came from the hand of the Creator, and was pronounced "good.". . . The order of Zion is such as will leave the earth as near its primordial, paradisiacal condition as possible. The paradise of Eden is called in the scriptures "the garden of the Lord" (Genesis 13:10), and we are told that God and his holy angels delighted to come to it and commune with Adam in its delightful surroundings.[19]

Zion people seek for beauty: "If there is anything virtuous, lovely, or of good report or praiseworthy, we seek after these things."[20] A Zion person is refined, modest, virtuous and beautiful beyond the charms of Babylon. A Zion person approaches and eventually exceeds the beauties of Eden. Such a person is described as blessed and beautiful: "And blessed are they who shall seek to bring forth my Zion at that day. . . . and whoso shall publish peace. . . . how beautiful upon the mountains shall they be."[21]

---

16 Psalms 50:2.
17 *American Heritage Dictionary*, s.v. "Beauty."
18 D&C 82:14.
19 Nibley, *Approaching Zion*, 7.
20 Thirteenth Article of Faith.
21 1 Nephi 13:37.

Becoming Unified—"Of One Heart and One Mind"

President Gordon B. Hinckley taught that cooperation exemplifies and empowers people who are striving to become Zionlike: "When you are united, your power is limitless. You can accomplish anything you wish to accomplish."[22] This phenomenon is called "synergy." That is, when two or more agents act together, they create an effect greater than the sum of the individual agents. For example, if one thread can hold five pounds, two threads woven together might actually hold twenty or more pounds!

Oneness is the divinely mandated goal for all covenant relationships: "I say unto you, be one; and if ye are not one ye are not mine."[23] Jesus exemplifies oneness by being "no respecter of persons"[24]; that is, he has equal regard for everyone, and likewise, he expects Zion people to be "even as I am."[25] The Godhead sets the example of unity: "The Father, and I, and the Holy Ghost are one."[26] Jesus commands Zion people to likewise become one with each other and one with the Father and with him: "That they all may be one; as thou, Father, art in me, and I in thee, that they also may be one in us . . . that they may be one, even as we are one: I in them, and thou in me, that they may be made perfect in one."[27]

Jesus wrought the infinite Atonement so that we might become one with the Father and with him. "The literal meaning of the word 'Atonement' is self-evident: at-one-ment, the act of unifying or bringing together what has been separated and estranged."[28] We cannot fully accept the Atonement without becoming one with each other and with the Father and the Son. The Savior taught the Nephites that Zion people become one by ending contention and disputations,[29] to deal justly with each other,[30] and by ending economic and social distinctions.[31] Zion-like oneness is manifested in the covenant marriage.[32] That is, God provided us the sealing power[33] to make us one—to "turn the heart of the fathers to the children, and the heart of the children to their fathers."[34]

The preeminent quality of oneness has always described Zion people: "And the Lord called his people Zion, because they were of one heart and one mind, and dwelt in righteousness; and there was no poor among them."[35] Divisiveness of any kind or in any degree is an invention of the devil[36] and thus characteristic of Babylon.

---

22 Hinckley, "Your Greatest Challenge, Mother," 97.
23 D&C 38:27.
24 D&C 38:16.
25 3 Nephi 27:27; D&C 38:27.
26 3 Nephi 11:36.
27 John 17:21–23.
28 *Encyclopedia of Mormonism,* s.v. "Atonement," 83.
29 3 Nephi 11:22–28.
30 4 Nephi 1:2–3.
31 3 Nephi 6:10–16; 4 Nephi 1:2–3, 24–35.
32 D&C 38:26–27.
33 D&C 132:19.
34 Malachi 4:6.
35 Moses 7:18.
36 3 Nephi 11:29.

Striving for Equality—"No Poor among Them"

The *Encyclopedia of Mormonism* explains, "Since love comprehends all righteousness (Matt. 22:36–40), the people of Zion live together in love as equals."[37] From the beginning of this dispensation, the Lord emphatically insisted that we strive to become equal: "But it is not given that one man should possess that which is above another, wherefore the world lieth in sin."[38] A tragedy of inequality is that "the abundance of the manifestations of the Spirit [are] withheld."[39]

The Lord's solution for all forms of inequality is Zion. Equality does not infringe on our ability to remain individual; neither does it suggest communal living or joint ownership of property. Rather, equality provides that each of us enjoys equal access to the resources consecrated to the Lord and his Church. That is, Zion people have "all things common among them."[40] The Lord explained the eternal order of common access: "And you are to be equal, or in other words, *you are to have equal claims on the properties,* for the benefit of managing the concerns of your stewardships, every man according to his wants and his needs, inasmuch as his wants are just—And all this for the benefit of the church of the living God, that every man may improve upon his talent, that every man may gain other talents, yea, even an hundred fold, to be cast into the Lord's storehouse, to become the common property of the whole church—Every man seeking the interest of his neighbor, and doing all things with an eye single to the glory of God. This order I have appointed to be an everlasting order unto you."[41] This is the celestial order of Zion, which allows us to "enjoy in this world the type of equality that defines relations between persons in the celestial world (D&C 78:4–8; 105:4–5).[42]

Zion *levels up* its people. The poor are exalted by means of the consecrated offerings of the rich, meaning those who have more time, talents, and means than they need: "And it is my purpose to provide for my saints, for all things are mine. But it must needs be done in mine own way; and behold this is the way that I, the Lord, have decreed to provide for my saints, that the poor shall be exalted, in that the rich are made low."[43] Consequently, a true Zion person allows no poor—no monetarily, emotionally, physically or spiritually poor—to experience want within his circle of influence.[44]

By truly loving "thy neighbor as thyself,"[45] a Zion person esteems his brother as himself. Repeating the principle twice for emphasis, the Lord states: "And let every man esteem his brother as himself, and practise virtue and holiness before me. *And again* I say unto you, let every man esteem his brother as himself."[46] There can be no mistaking the meaning of this commandment. By obeying it, a Zion person lends his support to the cause of Zion, a central goal of which is that the covenant people of God enjoy "all things in common."[47]

---

37 *Encyclopedia of Mormonism,* s.v. "Zion," 1625.
38 D&C 49:20.
39 D&C 70:14.
40 3 Ne 26:19; 4 Nephi 1:3.
41 D&C 82:17–20, emphasis added.
42 *Encyclopedia of Mormonism,* s.v. "Equality," 463.
43 D&C 104:15–16.
44 Moses 7:18.
45 Matthew 22:39.
46 D&C 38:24–25; emphasis added.
47 Acts 2:44.

Becoming Selfless and Giving Christian Service

President Spencer W. Kimball had much to say about Zion: "Zion is 'every man seeing the interest of his neighbor, and doing all things with an eye single to the glory of God.'"[48] And at another time, "Are we interested in what we can get or are we interested in what we can give? The Savior's life was one of unselfish service. The Savior's doctrine and gospel is one of selflessness."[49]

Continuing, President Kimball also stated, "selflessness brings Zion."[50] Selflessness is the hallmark of heaven and thus of Zion: "Heaven is a place, but also a condition . . . *It is selflessness.*"[51] The Zion attribute of selflessness engenders a celestial level of happiness: "Selflessness is a key to happiness and effectiveness; it is precious and must be preserved as a virtue that guarantees so many other virtues."[52] Explaining this, President Kimball said, "One of the differences between true joy and mere pleasure is that certain pleasures are realized only at the cost of someone else's pain. Joy, on the other hand, springs out of selflessness and service, and it benefits rather than hurts others."[53] President James E. Faust added, "Our search for happiness largely depends on the degree of righteousness we attain, *the degree of selflessness we acquire*, the amount and quality of service we render, and the inner peace that we enjoy."[54]

The Savior's parable of the good Samaritan exemplifies the selflessness of a Zion person. Here was a Zion individual, who, without prejudice, showed compassion on a stranger, stopped to minister to the injured man, "set him on his own beast, and brought him to an inn, and took care of him." Then the Samaritan paid for the man's ongoing treatment.[55] That attitude of generosity and selfless service shown to someone in need is quintessentially Zion. Whenever we serve "one of the least" of God's children, the Lord counts our service as if we had done that service unto him.[56] And because God can be in debt to no one, he rewards our service with an incredible return—"an hundredfold."[57] Truly, he is the most generous paymaster. Upon this principle of giving and receiving "with increase,"[58] Zion people prosper. President Marion G. Romney said, "You cannot give yourself poor in this work; you can only give yourself rich."[59]

---

48 Kimball, "Becoming the Pure in Heart," 79; D&C 82:19.
49 Kimball, Conference Report, October 1951, 87.
50 Kimball, *The Teachings of Spencer W. Kimball*, 363.
51 Kimball, *Faith Precedes the Miracle*, 264; emphasis added
52 Kimball, "My Beloved Sisters," 17–19.
53 Kimball, "President Kimball Speaks Out," 40.
54 Faust, *"Our Search for Happiness,"* 2; emphasis added.
55 Luke 10:33–37.
56 Matthew 25:40.
57 Matthew 19:29.
58 Packer, "The Candle of the Lord," 51.
59 Romney, "Welfare Services: The Savior's Program," 92.

Introduction   Portrait of a Zion Person

Exhibiting the Pure Love of Christ

President Joseph F. Smith said, "Charity, or love, is the greatest principle in existence."[60] On the principle of love—love of God and love of neighbor—"hang all the law and the prophets."[61] Like other principles, love ranges in quality from telestial to celestial, which type of love is called charity, "the pure love of Christ." This is the quality of love found in a Zion person. Because charity is perfect, celestial love, it "never faileth."[62]

Charity describes God: "God is love."[63] Because we are commanded to be perfect like him,[64] we must learn to love as he loves. The more we develop and exhibit charity, the more God-like and Zion-like we become. The Apostle John taught that the person who loves best knows God best: "Beloved, let us love one another: for love is of God; and every one that loveth is born of God, and knoweth God."[65]

What sets celestial love apart from terrestrial and telestial forms of love is its motivation: Charity is more concerned with what it *does* than what it *feels*. Therefore, the opposite of love is not hate but apathy.[66] Perhaps the best description of charity is found in 1 Corinthians 13:1–13 and Moroni 7:44–48. Here is a list of attributes as seen through the lens of a Zion person:

- A Zion person suffers long (endures a hardship or endures with someone during his or her hardship).
- A Zion person is kind.
- A Zion person does not envy.
- A Zion person is not vaunted up (does not boast).
- A Zion person is not puffed up (is not proud).
- A Zion person does not behave unseemly (act rudely).
- A Zion person seeks not his or her own (is not selfish).
- A Zion person is not easily provoked (keeps temper under control).
- A Zion person thinks no evil (focuses on the good).
- A Zion person does not rejoice in iniquity but rejoices in the truth (is not inclined toward evil, but embraces anything virtuous, lovely, of good report, or praiseworthy[67]).
- A Zion person bears all things (bears up under the weight of problems).
- A Zion person believes all things (recognizes and follows truth).
- A Zion person hopes all things (knows ultimately that God is in charge).
- A Zion person endures all things (is willing to pay the price because he knows the wait will be worth it).

---

60 Smith, Conference Report, April 1917, 4.
61 Matthew 22:40.
62 Moroni 7:46–47.
63 1 John 4:7–8.
64 Matthew 5:48.
65 1 John 4:7.
66 Ashton, "Be a Quality Person," 93.
67 Articles of Faith 13.

Charity (celestial, Zion-like love) differs from telestial and terrestrial manifestations of love by the fact that it is *saving* love. Charity lifts another person; charity has the capacity to forgive and rescue from enormous distances. As we give and receive this celestial love, we discover that those within our gravitational pull cannot escape our loving embrace.

Charity, the love of Zion, is built on the foundation of
1. total loyalty
2. total sacrifice
3. total trust

Moreover, charity has three manifestations:
1. love from Christ
2. love for Christ
3. love like Christ

Expounding, H. Wallace Goddard referenced Elder Max Caldwell, observing, "Charity is first and foremost the redemptive love that Jesus offers all of us. It is the love from Christ. He is the model of charity—which never faileth."[68]

When we receive love *from* Christ, we develop love *for* Christ. We might ask ourselves, "How does celestial love germinate?" And the answer would be: By Jesus' showing his love for us first. Both Heavenly Father and Jesus set the example: "Herein is love, not that we loved God, but that he loved us . . . We love him, because he first loved us."[69] Likewise, when we take the initiative and show love to someone first, that love is returned with an increase. It is an oft-repeated scriptural formula that has many applications. For example, "Blessed are the merciful: for they shall obtain mercy."[70] Elder Boyd K. Packer said it this way: "As you give what you have, there is a replacement, with increase!"[71] John Greenleaf Whittier wrote, "I'll lift you, and you lift me, and we'll both ascend together." This is the love of Zion.

Whereas Babylon elevates only *me*, Zion elevates others *through me*. Zion-like love is not only an expansive principle, it is one that draws God near to us and becomes perfect when we accept it and do not turn away from it.[72] The Apostle John said, "If we love one another, God dwelleth in us, and his love is perfected in us."[73] Moreover, by showing love through selfless service, we receive an added measure of the Holy Ghost: "Hereby know we that we dwell in him, and he in us, because he hath given us of his Spirit."[74] As we abide in this cycle of loving and receiving love, our ability to love eventually becomes perfect: "God is love; and he that dwelleth in love dwelleth in God, and God in him. Herein is our love made perfect."[75]

---

68 Goddard, *Drawing Heaven into Your Marriage*, 111.
69 1 John 4:10, 19.
70 Matthew 5:7.
71 Packer, "The Candle of the Lord," 51.
72 1 Nephi 8:28.
73 1 John 4:12.
74 1 John 4:13.
75 1 John 4:16–17.

Introduction   Portrait of a Zion Person

One of the greatest benefits of love is ceasing to be afraid: "There is no fear in love; but perfect love casteth out fear."[76]

Moreover, Zion-like love is patient, which means:
1. "I will wait *with* you."
2. "I will wait *for* you."
3. "I will wait *upon* you," meaning "I will serve you."

In one way or another, Zion-like love means *I will wait*.

Love—celestial Zion love—is the greatest power in the universe. It is the "Royal Law,"[77] which James quoted the Savior as defining: "Thou shalt love the Lord thy God with all thy heart, and with all thy soul, and with all thy mind. This is the first and great commandment. And the second is like unto it, Thou shalt love thy neighbour as thyself."[78]

Love motivates God to do all that he does.[79] The greatest expression of his love is to give and redeem life. He invites all of his children to experience this quality of love and his quality of life, for therein is his "joy made full."[80] By following his example—giving life and redeeming life—is our joy also made full.[81] And the words *full* and *fullness* always describe Zion.

---

76   1 John 4:18.
77   James 2:8.
78   Matthew 22:36–40.
79   Moses 1:39.
80   3 Nephi 17:20.
81   Alma 26:11, 16; 3 Nephi 27:31; 28:10.

Experiencing True Happiness, Joy, and the Fullness of Life

The scriptures associate happiness and joy with the fullness of life.[82] The Prophet Joseph Smith taught, "Happiness is the object and design of our existence; and will be the end thereof, if we pursue the path that leads to it; and this path is virtue, uprightness, faithfulness, holiness, and keeping all the commandments of God."[83]

Happiness, like other gospel principles, exists in varying degrees "ranging from 'celestial' to 'telestial,' depending on the level of 'law' [individuals] 'abide' (D&C 88:22–35; 76)."[84] People of Zion enjoy happiness on a level that approaches celestial. Having embraced the Covenant after the coming of Christ, the Nephites enjoyed happiness equal to that of Enoch's people. Elder Marion G. Romney described this group of Nephites as "a society in which, 'there was no contention . . . because of the love of God which did dwell in the hearts of the people'; a society in which, 'there were no envyings, nor strifes, nor tumults, nor whoredoms, nor lyings, nor murders, nor any manner of lasciviousness;' a society in which every member had conquered the lusts of the flesh. '. . . and surely,' concludes the record, *'there could not be a happier people among all the people who had been created by the hand of God.'* (4 Nephi 15–16)."[85] Certainly, the absence of evil promotes joy, but only "virtue, uprightness, faithfulness, holiness, and keeping all the commandments of God,"[86] which includes selfless service, facilitates true joy.[87] If the purpose of man's creation is that he might have joy,[88] then that man must develop these attributes in his character.

We experience joy, in part, by awareness and appreciation for "the gifts of life, the earth, and personal agency (e.g., taste, smell, beauty, music)"; by "using these gifts to create opportunities or to develop relationships (e.g., marriage, parenting, charity); by "coming to understand how mortality fits into the divine purpose or plan of Heavenly Father" (using this understanding "as a framework for comprehending and assimilating life's experiences"); and by "accepting Christ as Savior and feeling his acceptance and approval of one's efforts."[89]

Elder McConkie explained that only entering into the joy of the Lord[90] can result in a fullness of joy, which is the ultimate condition of Zion people. True happiness, or *joy*, he said, "is a gift of the Spirit. It comes from the Holy Ghost,"[91] suggesting that Satan cannot duplicate the feeling of joy. "In this connection, the Book of Mormon describes a scene wherein 'the spirit of the Lord came upon them, and they were filled with joy, having received a remission of their sins, and having peace of conscience' (Mosiah 4:3; cf.

---

82   4 Nephi 1:3, 16; Mosiah 16:11.
83   Smith, *Teachings of the Prophet Joseph Smith*, 255–56.
84   *Encyclopedia of Mormonism*, s.v. "Zion,"1625.
85   Marion G. Romney, Conference Report, April 1958, 126; emphasis added
86   Smith, *Teachings of the Prophet Joseph Smith*, 255–56.
87   Matthew 16:25; Mosiah 4:3, 20.
88   2 Nephi 2:25.
89   *Encyclopedia of Mormonism*, s.v. "Joy," 771.
90   D&C 51:19.
91   McConkie, *Mormon Doctrine*, "Joy," 397.

John 15:10–12)."[92] Therefore, the more faith-filled, repentant, humble, and Zion-like we become, the more joy we experience. Moreover, our seeking the establishment of Zion in our lives will serve to dispel sadness and result in the highest degree of joy: "For the Lord shall comfort Zion, he will comfort all her waste places; and he will make her wilderness like Eden, and her desert like the garden of the Lord. Joy and gladness shall be found therein, thanksgiving and the voice of melody."[93]

---

92 *Encyclopedia of Mormonism*, s.v. "Joy," 771.
93 2 Nephi 8:3.

Becoming Holy

Zion is a holy place—"the City of Holiness"[94]—whose individual citizens are holy: "he that is left in Zion . . . shall be called holy."[95] We cannot make ourselves holy; only God can do that.[96] Our responsibility is to strive for holiness by living the new and everlasting covenant, which has the power to bring us to perfection, and thus holiness. Because Zion "cannot be built up unless it is by the principles of the law of the celestial kingdom,"[97] a state of holiness is not possible unless we embrace this celestial Covenant and become like celestial people. Brigham Young explained the goal of holiness that is pursued by Zion people: "We are trying to be the image of those who live in heaven; we are trying to pattern after them, to look like them, to walk and talk like them, to deal like them, and build up the kingdom of heaven as they have done."[98]

Becoming holy is a journey: "The process of becoming holy is based on three doctrines: *justification*, which satisfies the demands of justice for the sins of the individual through the Atonement of Jesus Christ; *purification*, made possible by that same Atonement and symbolized in the sacrament of the bread and water, requiring the constant cleansing of oneself from earthly stains and imperfections; and *sanctification*, the process of being made holy. Having purified oneself of imperfections to the greatest degree possible, one is invested, over a lifetime, with holiness from God."[99]

The concept of perfection, the ultimate expression of holiness, can seem overwhelming to struggling mortals. This commandment is stated in the Sermon on the Mount. Using the Father as an example, Jesus told his disciples in Jerusalem: "Ye are therefore commanded to be perfect even as your Father which is in heaven is perfect."[100] Later, to the Nephites, he gave substantially the same commandment, but this time he added himself as an example: "Therefore I would that ye should be perfect even as I, or your Father who is in heaven is perfect."[101]

We see in these verses a subtle indication that total perfection is acquired by going from one *perfection* to another. While Jesus was in the flesh, although he was a perfect man, he was nevertheless not yet as perfect as his Father, who was now a resurrected, glorified man. But after Jesus' Resurrection, as indicated in his rewording the commandment to the Nephites, Jesus could claim the Father's quality of perfection. Clearly, this exalted level of perfection can only be attained *after* the Resurrection.

Interestingly, some gospel writers have suggested that the Savior's commandment to become perfect points to the diligence we give to abiding in the new and everlasting covenant. Hence, the verse might read, "Ye are therefore commanded to be perfect in living the Covenant even as your Father which is in heaven is perfect in living the

---

94   Moses 7:19.
95   Isaiah 4:3.
96   *Encyclopedia of Mormonism*, s.v. "Holiness," 648.
97   D&C 105:5.
98   *Journal of Discourses*, 9:170.
99   *Encyclopedia of Mormonism*, s.v. "Holiness," 648.
100 JST, Matthew 5:50.
101 3 Nephi 12:48.

Covenant." That is, with the same degree of diligence that the Father gives to perfectly abiding in the Covenant, we must strive to abide in the Covenant—"even unto death, that [we] may be found worthy."[102]

We do not arrive at this or any level of perfection automatically. Nevertheless, we understand that just men, who are not yet ultimately perfect, are nevertheless *made* perfect through the grace of Jesus Christ.[103] That is, abiding in the Covenant assures us the enabling power of the Atonement to make us *as if* we were perfect until the time that we are wholly perfect, meaning "finished, complete, fully developed."[104] Perhaps being made perfect by the grace of Jesus Christ is what is meant when we read of just men like Noah, who is described as perfect in his generation.[105] Likewise, we are *made* perfect in the Covenant, which is designed to move us forward to ultimate perfection and holiness, if we will abide in it as does our Father, whose name is Man of Holiness.[106]

Therefore, we have no reason to lose hope. The prophets have taught us repeatedly that it is our direction, not our arriving, that makes all the difference. The perfection of Enoch's Zion, we are told, happened in the "process of time."[107]

---

[102] D&C 98:14.
[103] Moroni 10:32–33; D&C 76:69; 129:3; Hebrews 12:23.
[104] Matthew 5:48 footnote *b*.
[105] Moses 8:27.
[106] Moses 6:57; 7:35.
[107] Moses 7:21.

Achieving the State of Blessedness

When Jesus appeared to the Nephites, he taught them the principles of *blessedness*, otherwise known as *Beatitudes*, which means "to be blessed" or "to be happy." Jesus had taught these same principles to his Judean disciples at the Sermon on the Mount[108] and later at Christ's sermon on the plain.[109] To the Nephites he added several additional principles of blessedness. Collectively, the body of principles contained in these two sermons could aptly be described as the law of the gospel.

President Harold B. Lee called this sermon "the constitution for a perfect life."[110] He wrote, "In order to gain entrance into the kingdom of Heaven, we must not only be good but we are required to do good and be good for something."[111] That is, we must strive to achieve the celestial state of blessedness that characterizes a Zion person. President Lee suggested that these principles of blessedness "represent a recipe for righteousness with incremental steps."[112]

The Beatitudes follow an intriguing sequence that leads from one state of blessedness to the next. In fact, they mark our spiritual journey from its inception to its perfect conclusion. Consider, for example, the soul who is poor in spirit. That he lacks pride is one interpretation, but another suggests that he is spiritually impoverished, lacking that which is essential to make the journey to the promised land. His spiritual lack draws him to the only Source; thus Jesus commends those who are poor in spirit "who come unto me," promising and prophesying that "theirs is the kingdom of heaven."[113] That is, the kingdom of heaven on earth—the Church of Jesus Christ, which is the custodian of saving covenants and ordinances—is the inheritance of those who humble themselves and make their way to Christ seeking to satisfy their spiritual lack. Then having received of the Spirit, the once-impoverished are strengthened to journey onward until they arrive in the celestial kingdom of heaven.

Recognition of spiritual lack also causes sons and daughters of God to mourn or mourn *righteously*—mourning that leads to spiritual growth. For whatever reason, sin, or weakness, they mourn for their fallen condition and plead for relief. The Lord responds to such mourning with comfort,[114] a soothing voice and soft touch, and the promise of eventual reward.

Spiritual lack and righteous mourning summon meekness, that Godlike quality of humility. The meek yearn to ascend from their spiritual poverty and reduced circumstances and yearn to be reunited and reconciled with God and enjoy spiritual abundance. Their longings are heard by the Lord throught prayers, and those prayers are answered again with the promise of inheritance: this time inheritance of the earth,[115] which shall become a celestial kingdom.[116]

---

108 Matthew 5–7.
109 Luke 6:20–49.
110 Lee, *Decisions for Successful Living*, 56–57.
111 Lee, *Decisions for Successful Living*, 59–60.
112 Condie, "Agency: The Gift of Choices," 16.
113 3 Nephi 12:3.
114 3 Nephi 12:4.
115 D&C 45:58.
116 D&C 88:18–26.

Spiritual lack, righteous mourning, meekness—what do they lead to? "Hungering and thirsting after righteousness."[117] Who is the Righteous? Jesus Christ.[118] What are His names? The Bread of Life;[119] the Living Water.[120] What is the promise given to those who hunger and thirst for the Bread of Life, the Living Water, the Righteous? "They shall be filled with the Holy Ghost."[121] "And Jesus said unto them, I am the bread of life: he that cometh to me shall never hunger; and he that believeth on me shall never thirst."[122]

When a person receives the miracles of the Lord—being relieved of spiritual poverty, experiencing divine comfort, being spiritually fed—he realizes that he has been blessed by love alone, not for any deserving action. The miracle is a pure manifestation of mercy. Then another miracle occurs when the recipient discovers that mercy is both an expansive and a reciprocal principle: mercy grows and returns by giving mercy. Thus the Lord promises that those who give away the mercy they received from the Lord will yet see that mercy, compounded, return again to them. "And blessed are the merciful, for they shall obtain mercy."[123]

The acts of mercy-giving and mercy-receiving tend to purify the soul. Eventually, they who are sufficiently purified—"the pure in heart"—shall, with an immutable promise, "see God."[124] This is the end of the journey for those who have struggled to overcome their spiritual impoverishment, mourned for their fallen condition, humbled themselves before the Lord, hungered and thirsted to find Him and know all about Him, lived as He lives: extending mercy as they receive mercy, and submitting to the purifying process of the Holy Ghost— "*all* the pure in heart . . . shall see God."

What do the pure in heart become? *Peacemakers*—makers of peace in similitude of the Prince of Peace. They abhor contentions and disputations; they do the peaceable works of Christ. Their promise is glorious: "They shall be called the children of God;"[125] that is, they become the sons and daughters not only by descendency but by spiritual birth and inheritance: heirs of salvation.[126]

The state of the pure in heart and peacemakers places them at odds with Babylon. Suddenly, the sons and daughters of God find themselves at war with a system that will no longer support them. This intense hatred summons persecution in a multitude of ways. Lehi and Nephi listed a few: mockery, scorn, anti-Christ philosophies, direct or overt conditions that tend to "yoke, torture, slay, and bind." Who are the persecutors? The idolaters, the materialistic, and the spiritually perverse, to name a few.[127] The Lord reserves great promises for those who endure the word's persecution: "For ye shall have great joy and be exceedingly glad, for great shall be your reward in heaven."[128]

---

117 3 Nephi 12:6.
118 Moses 7:47.
119 John 6:48.
120 John 4:11.
121 3 Nephi 12:6.
122 John 6:35.
123 3 Nephi 12:7.
124 3 Nephi 12:8.
125 3 Nephi 12:9.
126 Mosiah 27:25; D&C 25:1.
127 1 Nephi 8:26–28; 13:7–9.
128 3 Nephi 12:10–12.

Clearly, the Beatitudes mark the spiritual journey that begins with the first motions of conversion and ends with unequalled celestial reward. They describe what we become by following this journey.

Let us take a further view involving other or more in-depth interpretations of the Beatitudes through the lens of becoming a Zion person.

Sustaining Leaders

"Blessed are ye if ye shall give heed unto the words of these twelve whom I have chosen from among you to minister unto you."[129] A Zion person sustains his rank and file leaders and covenants to live by their counsel. A Zion person recognizes the Lord's voice in the voice of his servants: "Whether by mine own voice or by the voice of my servants, it is the same."[130]

Interestingly, when we sustain our leaders, we do so with the right hand, which is the sign of covenant-making. Our keeping this sustaining covenant promotes the oneness demanded by Zion, and it allows the Spirit to flow through our leaders to us—an avenue of revelation that is vital to our spiritual survival and progression. Clearly, through the servants of God, Zion people are blessed.

Believing Christ by Receiving Baptism and the Holy Ghost

"Blessed are ye if ye shall believe in me and be baptized . . . behold, I will baptize you with fire and with the Holy Ghost."[131] This principle of blessedness hearkens to the first principles and ordinances of the gospel: faith in Jesus Christ, repentance, baptism, and receiving the Holy Ghost.[132] Only faith in Jesus Christ—believing who he is and what he has done—can motivate a person to seek a change of heart,[133] symbolized and formalized by baptism, the "covenant of salvation."[134] Baptism is the gate that one passes through to leave and be saved from Babylon (a type of hell) and to enter the path leading to Zion (a type of the celestial kingdom).

Baptism by water and baptism by the Spirit are equally essential. Joseph Smith said, "Baptism by water is but half a baptism, and is good for nothing without the other half—that is, the baptism of the Holy Ghost."[135] Elder McConkie listed the four purposes for baptism. These purposes are: 1) baptism is for the remission of sins; 2) baptism gives the repentant person membership in the Church and admits him into the kingdom of God on earth; 3) baptism is the gate to the celestial kingdom of heaven; that is, it starts a person out on the straight and narrow path which leads to eternal life; and 4) baptism is the means whereby the door to personal sanctification is opened.[136]

---

129 3 Nephi 12:1; emphasis added.
130 D&C 1:38.
131 3 Nephi 12:1; emphasis added.
132 Articles of Faith 4.
133 Alma 5:7, 13–15.
134 McConkie, "Baptism," *Mormon Doctrine*, 69–72.
135 Smith, *Teachings of the Prophet Joseph Smith*, 314.
136 McConkie, *Mormon Doctrine*, "Baptism," 69–72.

Jesus commanded, "Repent, all ye ends of the earth, and come unto me and be baptized in my name that ye may be sanctified by the reception of the Holy Ghost that ye may stand spotless before me at the last day."[137] One of the criteria of the baptismal covenant especially points us to Zion: "to bear one another's burdens, that they may be light."[138]

Bearing Testimony

"Blessed are they who shall believe in your words."[139] Someone hearing the testimony of a Zion person is blessed because he has heard and believed the word of God on faith alone.[140] Likewise, the Zion person who has borne testimony is blessed by having his testimony recorded in heaven and by receiving anew a remission of sins: "Nevertheless, ye are blessed, for the testimony which ye have borne is recorded in heaven for the angels to look upon; and they rejoice over you, and your sins are forgiven you."[141]

The blessedness that is inherent in a Zion person draws others to him by means of his spoken or unspoken testimony. Bearing testimony makes a Zion person the "salt of the earth," and salt, of course, is a "healing, flavoring, and preserving agent."[142] By means of his testimony and service, a Zion person "succors the weak, lifts up the hands which hang down, and strengthens the feeble knees."[143] Additionally, bearing testimony characterizes Zion's blessedness by making a Zion person a light to the world: "Verily, verily, I say unto you, I give unto you to be the light of this people. . . . Therefore let your light so shine before this people, that they may see your good works and glorify your Father who is in heaven."[144]

Becoming Poor in Spirit

"Yea, blessed are the poor in spirit who come unto me, for theirs is the kingdom of heaven."[145] A common interpretation of this phrase is "blessed are the poor in pride, or the poor of this world." That is, a person who is poor in spirit lacks pride. Perhaps he is devoid of pride because he has not enjoyed the things of this world; or maybe he lacks pride because he has disciplined himself to not set his heart on the things of this world; then again, he might lack pride because he is in need of additional spiritual insight or strength. In any case, when such people recognize their need or weakness and come to Christ, the Lord will "make weak things become strong unto them."[146] This enabling principle is called *grace*,[147] and it demonstrates the strength of *oneness* we gain when we partner with the Lord in the Covenant. In that partnership, the weak (poor

---

137 3 Nephi 27:20.
138 Mosiah 18:8.
139 3 Nephi 12:2; emphasis added.
140 John 20:29.
141 D&C 62:3.
142 Largey, ed., *The Book of Mormon Reference Companion*, s.v. "Salt," 695.
143 D&C 81:5.
144 3 Nephi 12:14, 16.
145 3 Nephi 12:3, emphasis added.
146 Ether 12:27.
147 Bible Dictionary, s.v. "Grace" 697.

in spirit) person yokes himself to Christ[148] and thereby becomes as strong as his Companion. Therefore, it is with great eagerness that a Zion person is willing to declare his nothingness and vulnerability, and seek the Lord with full dependency,[149] rather than relying on the arm of flesh, or his own genius and strength.[150]

The associated blessings are remarkable: "And behold, I say unto you that if ye do this ye shall always rejoice, and be filled with the love of God, and always retain a remission of your sins; and ye shall grow in the knowledge of the glory of him that created you, or in the knowledge of that which is just and true."[151] In this sense, being poor in spirit is a redeeming quality.

Considered in another light, our being poor in spirit can suggest a deficit of character that needs correcting. Therefore, the poor in spirit who admit their sins, "viewing themselves in their own carnal state, even less than the dust of the earth," and repent, crying, "O have mercy, and apply the atoning blood of Christ that we may receive forgiveness of our sins, and our hearts may be purified; for we believe in Jesus Christ, the Son of God";[152] those who yearn for forgiveness, strip themselves of pride, and come to the Lord in humility seeking the return of the Spirit, will be filled with the Holy Ghost. They will be "filled with joy, having received a remission of their sins, and having peace of conscience, because of the exceeding faith which they had in Jesus Christ."[153]

Mourning Righteously

"Blessed are all they that mourn, for they shall be comforted."[154] Notice the word *all*. When a person who is poor is spirit (pride) comes to the Lord, and when the Lord shows the person his weakness, that person *mourns*, which, interestingly, can be an act of worship.[155] The characteristic of one who mourns is having a broken heart and a contrite spirit.[156] He recognizes his nothingness and carnal nature and longs for support and deliverance.

When the people of King Benjamin made this discovery, they immediately shed themselves of pride, came to Christ, and mourned, desiring desperately to be delivered from Babylon and brought into Zion: "And they had viewed themselves in their own carnal state, even less than the dust of the earth. And they all cried aloud with one voice, saying: O have mercy, and apply the atoning blood of Christ that we may receive forgiveness of our sins, and our hearts may be purified; for we believe in Jesus Christ, the Son of God, who created heaven and earth, and all things; who shall come down among the children of men."[157]

---

148 Matthew 11:29.
149 Mosiah 4:11.
150 Alma 30:17.
151 Mosiah 4:12.
152 Mosiah 4:2.
153 Mosiah 4:3.
154 3 Nephi 12:3.
155 Alma 30:2; Helaman 9:10; D&C 95:7.
156 3 Nephi 9:20; 12:19.
157 Mosiah 4:2.

Righteous mourning is characteristic of a Zion person, whose compassion demands that he "mourns with those who mourn."[158] Such empathetic mourning stems from and leads to feelings of compassion, kindness, and mercy. A Zion person feels genuine sorrow for those who suffer, and he is moved to exhibit tenderness and loving assistance toward them; he strives "to bear one another's burdens, that they may be light . . . and comfort those that stand in need of comfort."[159] Jesus set the example: "And he said unto them: Behold, my bowels are filled with compassion towards you. Have ye any that are sick among you? Bring them hither. Have ye any that are lame, or blind, or halt, or maimed, or leprous, or that are withered, or that are deaf, or that are afflicted in any manner? Bring them hither and I will heal them, for I have compassion upon you; my bowels are filled with mercy."[160]

A person who mourns for his own sins, the death of a loved one, or whose mourning moves him to compassion[161] so that he is willing to "bear with or suffer with"[162] someone in need, is promised consolation from the Comforter. Eventually, his sorrow shall be turned into joy.[163] This is the condition of Zion.

Becoming Meek

"And blessed are the meek, for they shall inherit the earth."[164] To be meek is to be gentle, humble, patient, and submissive.[165] But meekness is not weakness; nevertheless Babylon perceives meekness as such and often persecutes it.[166] President Lee said, "A meek man . . . is not easily provoked or irritated and forbearing under injury or annoyance."[167] President Hinckley said, "The meek and the humble are those who are teachable. They are willing to learn. They are willing to listen to the whisperings of the still, small voice for guidance in their lives. They place the wisdom of the Lord above their own wisdom."[168]

Meekness is a childlike quality[169] that the Savior attributed to himself.[170] A person who is meek is often described as being lowly in heart; that is, by his true penitence, he is ready "to hear the word of the Lord."[171] Thus, a person who exercises faith in Christ, humbles himself, repents, and accepts baptism, receives a remission of his sins, which "bringeth meekness, and lowliness of heart; and because of meekness and lowliness of heart cometh the visitation of the Holy Ghost, which Comforter filleth with hope and perfect love."[172]

---

158 Mosiah 18:9.
159 Mosiah 18:8–9.
160 3 Nephi 17:6–7.
161 Matthew 9:36.
162 Ogden and Skinner, *Verse by Verse: The Four Gospels*, 177.
163 John 16:20.
164 3 Nephi 12:6.
165 *American Heritage Dictionary*, s.v. "Meek."
166 2 Nephi 9:30; 28:13; Helaman 6:39.
167 Lee, *Decisions for Successful Living*, 60.
168 Hinckley, *Stand a Little Taller*, 18.
169 Mosiah 3:19.
170 Matthew 11:29.
171 Largey, ed. *Book of Mormon Reference Companion*, "Lowliness of Heart," 524.
172 Moroni 8:26.

Those who are meek and lowly of heart "find rest to their souls,"[173] which rest is the glory of the Lord.[174] They receive the knowledge and the love of God and know that they are right before him.[175] One must become meek and lowly of heart before he can obtain the spiritual gifts of faith, hope and charity; to live otherwise is in vain, "for none is acceptable before God, save the meek and lowly in heart."[176]

It is the attribute of meekness that gives us access to the Lord's grace,[177] that help or strength that is beyond our ability, which is proffered to us through the love and mercy of Jesus Christ.[178] A Zion person strives to become meek and lowly of heart, "humble, patient, full of love, willing to submit to all things which the Lord seeth fit to inflict upon him, even as a child doth submit to his father."[179] The Lord's promise to such a person is that he will gain an eternal inheritance on the earth,[180] which will become Zion and a celestial kingdom to those who live on it.[181]

Hungering and Thirsting after [for] Righteousness

"And blessed are all they who do hunger and thirst after righteousness, for they shall be filled with the Holy Ghost."[182] Again, notice the word *all*.

The Lord taught us that everything has spiritual underpinnings,[183] therefore all hunger, including physical hunger, can be traced to a corresponding spiritual need. Therefore, we might venture that to be physically or spiritually hungry and thirsty is designed to lead us to Christ, the Bread of Life and the Living Water.[184] Whereas physical hunger motivates the need for food, spiritual hunger motivates the need for redemption. If we will allow physical hungers their purpose, they will usher us to Christ.

Only Jesus can provide spiritual nourishment for a starved, parched spirit. His solution is an infusion of the Spirit: "Blessed are all they who do hunger and thirst after righteousness, for they shall be filled with the Holy Ghost."[185] When we consume the food and drink the Holy Ghost gives, our appetite increases and we long for more. Then, as we continue to hunger and thirst for righteousness, we receive the eventual promise: *fulfillment*; that is, we are filled. "The Greek word [*filled*] . . . originally meant to feed and fatten an animal. It carried the notion of eating till one was completely and totally satisfied. Such is the Lord's promise to those who hunger and thirst after righteousness. He will feed us more than we can possibly imagine."[186]

---

173 Alma 37:33–34.
174 D&C 84:24.
175 Smith, ed., *Gospel Doctrine*, 5th ed., 58, 125–126.
176 Moroni 7:43–44.
177 Ether 12:26–27.
178 Bible Dictionary, s.v. "Grace," 697.
179 Mosiah 3:19.
180 3 Nephi 12:5.
181 D&C 88:17–26; 130:9.
182 3 Nephi 12:7.
183 D&C 29:34.
184 John 6:35; John 4:10.
185 3 Nephi 12:6.
186 Ogden and Skinner, *Verse by Verse: The Four Gospels*, 178–79.

This promise hearkens to the quality of abundance found in Zion—no lack of any good thing. Jesus demonstrated the spiritual principle of completely satisfying hunger and thirst when he fed the Israelites with manna for forty years,[187] when he fed Elijah by means of ravens,[188] when he fed the five thousand and later the four thousand,[189] and when he fed the Nephites at his appearance.[190]

A manifestation of hungering, thirsting and being filled is the law of the fast. This law offers us specific blessings: "to loose the bands of wickedness, to undo the heavy burdens, and to let the oppressed go free, and that ye break every yoke."[191] A true fast includes Zion-like selfless service: "to deal thy bread to the hungry, and that thou bring the poor that are cast out to thy house . . . when thou seest the naked, that thou cover him."[192] And it includes improving or reestablishing family relationships: "and that thou hide not thyself from thine own flesh."[193]

The blessings of the fast are amazing and singular—light, health, righteousness, protection, revelation: "Then shall thy light break forth as the morning, and thine health shall spring forth speedily: and thy righteousness shall go before thee; the glory of the Lord shall be thy rereward [guardian]. Then shalt thou call, and the LORD shall answer; thou shalt cry, and he shall say, Here I am."[194]

A true fast includes extending mercy ("tak[ing] away the yoke"), repenting, and giving selfless service: "draw out thy soul to the hungry, and satisfy the afflicted soul." Incredible blessings follow a true fast. The Lord will multiply your light, dispel the darkness that holds you captive, guide you continually, fill you spiritually and physically, bless your family forever with the gospel and priesthood, and bless you to become a savior and peacemaker to your family and to others. You become a "repairer of the breach."[195]

Likewise, we experience spiritual fulfillment when we go to the house of worship hungering and thirsting for righteousness and partake of the sacrament.[196] The sacrament is key to always being filled with the Spirit. Whereas we are given the gift of the Holy Ghost at our confirmation, we are guaranteed the Holy Ghost's ongoing companionship by means of the sacramental covenant. Having the Spirit perpetually with us points us toward eternal life.[197] If the Spirit is with us, we are deemed free from sin,[198] because the Spirit cannot dwell in an unclean tabernacle.[199] Therefore,

---

187 Exodus 16:32.
188 1 Kings 17:4.
189 Mark 6:35–44 and Mark 8:1–9.
190 3 Nephi 20:6–9.
191 Isaiah 58:6.
192 Isaiah 58:7.
193 Isaiah 58:7.
194 Isaiah 58:8–9.
195 Isaiah 58:9–12 "Then shall thy light rise in obscurity, and thy darkness be as the noonday: And the Lord shall guide thee continually, and satisfy thy soul in drought, and make fat thy bones: and thou shalt be like a watered garden, and like a spring of water, whose waters fail not. And they that shall be of thee shall build the old waste places: thou shalt raise up the foundations of many generations; and thou shalt be called, The repairer of the breach, The restorer of paths to dwell in."
196 Mosiah 18:7–10.
197 D&C 20:75–79; Moroni 4, 5.
198 Alma 34:36.
199 Alma 7:21; 1 Corinthians 3:16–17.

by the continual presence of the Holy Ghost, we are "made perfect,"[200] through the Atonement and merits of Jesus Christ.[201] That is the condition of Zion people.

Becoming Merciful

"And blessed are the merciful, for they shall obtain mercy."[202] The law of the harvest states, "Whatsoever ye sow, that shall ye also reap."[203] Applied to mercy, the law of the harvest reads, "Those who sow righteousness reap mercy."[204] That is, when a Zion person strives to live faithfully in the Covenant, he qualifies for the Lord's mercy.

Mercy is another of the gospel's reciprocal principles; once mercy is given it returns "with increase."[205] Mercy, like love, multiplies when it is "given first."[206] Elder Henry D. Moyle said, "There is an eternal truth, the verity of which I am certain, that love begets love, and as we love one another, our ability to love increases."[207] The same could be said of mercy. Pres Hinckley said, "How godlike a quality is mercy. It cannot be legislated. It must come from the heart. It must be stirred up from within. It is part of the endowment each of us receives as a son or daughter of God and partaker of a divine birthright. . . . I am convinced that there comes a time, possibly many times, within our lives when we might cry out for mercy on the part of others. How can we expect it unless we have been merciful ourselves? . . . One cannot be merciful to others without receiving a harvest of mercy in return."[208]

Mercy is defined as compassionate treatment, especially of those for whom we have a responsibility; it is showing clemency or leniency toward an offender; it is a disposition to be kind and forgiving, and it is exemplified by a willingness to alleviate distress and give relief.[209] Heavenly Father sets the standard of mercy: "Be ye therefore merciful, as your Father is also merciful."[210]

The Father's plan of mercy called for an infinite Atonement to "satisfy the demands of justice," and to encircle us "in arms of safety."[211] The Savior's mission was to enact the Father's plan of mercy, which "overpowereth justice, and bringeth about means unto men that they might have faith unto repentance."[212] Because of the Lord's Atonement, the meek have claim upon mercy: "I, the Lord, show mercy unto all the meek."[213] A Zion person is merciful even as the Lord is merciful.[214]

---

200 D&C 76:69.
201 Moroni 6:4.
202 3 Nephi 12:7.
203 D&C 6:33.
204 Hosea 10:12.
205 Packer, "The Candle of the Lord," 51.
206 1 John 4:19.
207 Moyle, Conference Report, April 1951, 125–126.
208 Hinckley, "Blessed are the Merciful," 68.
209 *American Heritage Dictionary,* s.v. "Mercy."
210 Luke 6:36.
211 Alma 34:15–16.
212 Alma 34:15–16.
213 D&C 97:2.
214 3 Nephi 27:27.

Introduction   Portrait of a Zion Person

Becoming Pure in Heart

"And blessed are all the pure in heart, for they shall see God."[215] Once again we note the inclusive word *all*. Perhaps this beatitude best describes a Zion person, for truly, "Zion is the pure in heart."[216]

President Kimball taught, "Zion can be built up only among those who are the pure in heart, not a people torn by covetousness or greed, but a pure and selfless people. Not a people who are pure in appearance, rather a people who are pure in heart. Zion is to be in the world and not of the world, not dulled by a sense of carnal security, nor paralyzed by materialism. No, Zion is not things of the lower, but of the higher order, things that exalt the mind and sanctify the heart."[217] President Kimball suggested three fundamental qualifications to become pure in heart and thus "bring again Zion."[218] These qualifications are: 1) eliminate selfishness, 2) cooperate completely and work in harmony one with one another, and 3) lay on the altar whatever is required by the Lord.[219]

To be pure in heart suggests a change of heart, or a rebirth, which begins with baptism and leads to eternal life: "Except a man be born of water and of the Spirit, he cannot enter into the kingdom of God."[220] Explaining the process of rebirth, or changing one's heart, the *Encyclopedia of Mormonism* states, "Scripture describes the rebirth to which Jesus refers as a 'mighty change in your hearts' or being 'born of God' (Alma 5:13, 14). It means that the person puts off the 'natural man' [telestial man] and puts on a new [Zion] nature that has 'no more disposition to do evil, but to do good continually' (Mosiah 5:2; 3:19). A person who is pure of heart is one who has died to evil and awakened to good. Thus 'pure people,' being alive to good, dwell together in righteousness and are called Zion (Moses 7:18). Zion, then, is the way of life of a pure-hearted people who abide in the Covenant and live the gospel of Jesus Christ."[221]

Beyond this description, the pure in heart are those who forsake their sins, come unto Christ, call on his name, obey his voice, and keep his commandments.[222] On August 2, 1833, the Lord gave an expanded revelation on the principle of being pure in heart: "And inasmuch as my people build a house unto me in the name of the Lord, and do not suffer any unclean thing to come into it, that it be not defiled, my glory shall rest upon it; Yea, and my presence shall be there, for I will come into it, and all the pure in heart that shall come into it shall see God."[223] This revelation places the temple at the center of importance concerning a pure-hearted person's qualifying to see God. "To see God, according to Elder Royden G. Derrick, [is more than visual sight; it] means to come to know God, discover him, and understand

---

215 3 Nephi 12:8.
216 D&C 97:21.
217 Kimball, *The Teachings of Spencer W. Kimball*, 363.
218 Isaiah 52:8; Mosiah 12:22; 15:29; 3 Nephi 16:18; D&C 113:8.
219 Kimball, *The Teachings of Spencer W. Kimball*, 363.
220 John 3:5.
221 *Encyclopedia of Mormonism*, s.v. "Zion,"1625.
222 D&C 93:1.
223 D&C 97:15–16.

him (*Temples in the Last Days*, 80)."[224] A Zion person is privileged to come to know God, discover him, understand him, and to literally see him, for Zion is God's "abode forever."[225]

The temple ordinances help to purify one's heart and point that person toward this supernal experience: "And this greater priesthood administereth the gospel and holdeth the key of the mysteries of the kingdom, even the key of the knowledge of God. Therefore, in the ordinances thereof [the ordinances of the Melchizedek Priesthood], the power of godliness is manifest. And without the ordinances thereof, and the authority of the priesthood, the power of godliness is not manifest unto men in the flesh; *For without this no man can see the face of God, even the Father, and live.* Now this Moses plainly taught to the children of Israel in the wilderness, and sought diligently to sanctify his people *that they might behold the face of God.*"[226]

And the temple is the likely place where that will happen.

Hugh Nibley said, "The temple is the earthly type of Zion."[227] Quite literally, the temple is heaven on earth. Because heaven is where God lives, the pure in heart—*all* the pure in heart[228]—may enter the temple, God's house and partake of its ordinances and commune with and someday see God.

Becoming A Maker of Peace

"And blessed are all the peacemakers, for they shall be called the children of God."[229] Again, notice the word *all* in this beatitude. Jesus said, "Peace I leave with you, my peace I give unto you: not as the world giveth, give I unto you."[230] Clearly, peace ranges in levels, as do other gospel principles, from telestial, which is almost non-existent[231] and usually means absence of war, to celestial, which "passeth all understanding."[232]

According to Elder McConkie, the Lord's peace is a gift of the Spirit,[233] and Satan cannot duplicate it.[234] Mortal fear flees in the face of the Lord's peace: "Let not your heart be troubled, neither let it be afraid."[235] When the Lord established Zion among the Nephites, they experienced unequalled peace. The following description is remarkable:

- No contentions
- No disputations

---

224 Ogden and Skinner, *Verse by Verse: The Four Gospels*, 180.
225 Moses 7:21.
226 D&C 84:19–23, insertion and emphasis added.
227 Nibley, *Approaching Zion*, 27.
228 3 Nephi 12:8.
229 3 Nephi 12:9.
230 John 14:27.
231 D&C 1:35.
232 Philippians 4:7.
233 McConkie, *Mormon Doctrine*, "Peace," 561–63. He lists the following scriptures: Psalms 37:37; 119:165; Isaiah 26:3; 48:18, 22; 57:21; Romans 8:6; 10:15; 14:17–19; 1 Corinthians 14:33; Ephesians 6:15.
234 George D. Watt, ed., *Journal of Discourses* 15:379; Sheri L. Dew, "Living on the Lord's Side of the Line," Brigham Young University devotional, March 21, 2000.
235 John 14:27.

- Every man dealing justly one with another
- All things in common
- No rich, poor, bond, or free
- Peace and prosperity in the land
- A love of God in the hearts of the people
- No envyings, strifes, tumults, whoredoms, lyings, murders, or lasciviousness
- No robbers, murderers, or any "-ites."[236]

Every person—*each and every peacemaker*[237]—who strives to make celestial peace follows the example of the Prince of Peace, and that person's reward is glorious: "He who doeth the works of righteousness shall receive his reward, even peace in this world, and eternal life in the world to come."[238] Melchizedek, who established Zion among his people, became a peacemaker and followed the example of the Savior in becoming a prince of peace: "Melchizedek did establish peace in the land in his days; therefore he was called the prince of peace."[239] Likewise, Abraham desired to establish Zion and become a prince of peace.[240]

The peace of Zion a peacemaker establishes blesses his family: "And all thy children shall be taught of the Lord; and great shall be the peace of thy children."[241] For making such an effort, the Lord promises that peacemakers will become sons and daughters of God, meaning that such people will become "joint heirs with Christ, inheriting with him the fullness of the Father. (D&C 93:17-23) . . . [and become] gods in eternity. (D&C 76:58)."[242]

Being Willing to Suffer Persecution for the Cause of Christ

"And blessed are all they who are persecuted for my name's sake, for theirs is the kingdom of heaven. And blessed are ye when men shall revile you and persecute, and shall say all manner of evil against you falsely, for my sake; For ye shall have great joy and be exceedingly glad, for great shall be your reward in heaven; for so persecuted they the prophets who were before you."[243] Persecution comes in a variety of ways, but it appears to be the common lot of every Saint who espouses the principles of Zion. Paul said, "All that will live godly in Christ Jesus shall suffer persecution."[244]

One form of persecution is mockery and scorn, as exhibited by the people in Lehi's great and spacious building: "Their manner of dress was exceedingly fine; and they were in the attitude of mocking and pointing their fingers towards those who had come and were partaking of the fruit."[245] That persecution grew out of

---

236 4 Nephi 1:15–17.
237 3 Nephi 12:10
238 D&C 59:23.
239 Alma 13:18.
240 Abraham 1:2.
241 Isaiah 59:23.
242 McConkie, *Mormon Doctrine*, "Son of God," 745.
243 3 Nephi 12:10–12.
244 2 Timothy 3:12.
245 1 Nephi 8:26.

the mockers' pride and vain imaginations, meaning their useless pursuits.[246] Those people were clearly vicious in their motive to dissuade the people of God.

Nephi described the philosophies of the persecutors as having the capacity to torture, slay, bind down, yoke, and bring into captivity the Saints of God.[247] We understand the meaning to include temporal and spiritual abuse and confinement. Such persecutors were idolaters, those who were materialistic, and the sexually perverse: "And I also saw gold, and silver, and silks, and scarlets, and fine-twined linen, and all manner of precious clothing; and I saw many harlots."[248]

The proud of Babylon, or the world, have always persecuted Zion's people, who are defined as the poor, i.e., poor in pride, poor in spirit, poor as to things of this world: "The wicked in his pride doth persecute the poor."[249] Moreover, they who are rich often judge the poor harshly and withhold their assistance, which is a form of persecution.[250] Additionally, they see themselves as part of an elevated class and consider themselves better than others.[251] Or they persecute, mock, and ignore the poor in favor of increasing their holdings, which they idolize as if they were sanctuaries: "Because of pride they are puffed up. They rob the poor because of their fine sanctuaries; they rob the poor because of their fine clothing; and they persecute the meek and the poor in heart, because in their pride they are puffed up."[252] This sin, according to Jacob, is "abominable unto God."[253]

Zion people are never accepted by Babylon, and they never will be. Babylon has been and ever will be the enemy and persecutor of Zion: "Know ye not that the friendship of the world is enmity with God? Whosoever therefore will be a friend of the world is the enemy of God."[254] For enduring the persecutions of Babylon, the humble followers of Christ will earn the greatest reward that God has to offer. Because they have believed in him and tried at all costs through their works and examples to build up his kingdom on the earth for the establishment of his Zion, they will inherit nothing less than the celestial kingdom of heaven, the eternal Zion of God.

These qualities are the conditions and characteristics of blessedness embraced and enjoyed by a Zion person. Some of these things speak eloquently to the first commandment to love God, while other qualities are encompassed in the second commandment to love our neighbor. These qualities are "Jesus' character in words,"[255] which President Harold B. Lee called the "constitution for a perfect life."[256] In every way, the Beatitudes describe Zion people.

---

246 1 Nephi 11:36.
247 1 Nephi 13:5.
248 1 Nephi 13:7.
249 Psalms 10:2.
250 Mosiah 4:17.
251 Jacob 2:13, 20.
252 2 Nephi 28:13.
253 Jacob 2:5.
254 James 4:4.
255 Ogden and Skinner, *Verse by Verse: The Four Gospels*, 173.
256 Lee, *Decisions for Successful Living*, 56–57.

Experiencing True Safety and Security

From the moment we declare our allegiance to Zion, Babylon will cry, "Treason!"[257] Then Babylon will withdraw her support from us and declare that we are enemies. At these times of trial, the Lord's promises of protection for Zion-like people are comforting. The following scriptures can be personalized.

"[Zion is] a city of refuge, a place of safety for the saints of the Most High God; And the glory of the Lord shall be there, and the terror of the Lord also shall be there, insomuch that the wicked will not come unto it, and it shall be called Zion . . . And it shall be said among the wicked: Let us not go up to battle against Zion, for the inhabitants of Zion are terrible; wherefore we cannot stand."[258] On a more personal and local note, Zion is a home, a place of refuge.

God protects Zion people from the perils of the world: "And all that fight against Zion [you and your family] shall be destroyed."[259] And on another occasion: "Verily, thus saith the Lord unto you—there is no weapon that is formed against you shall prosper; And if any man lift his voice against you he shall be confounded in mine own due time."[260]

The Lord has promised that the homes of latter-day Zion people will receive the same protection he extended to the ancient Israelites: "And the Lord will create upon every dwelling-place of mount Zion, and upon her assemblies, a cloud and smoke by day and the shining of a flaming fire by night; for upon all the glory of Zion shall be a defence."[261]

No danger is greater than the power of God: "Therefore, let your hearts be comforted concerning Zion [you and your family]; for all flesh is in mine hands; be still and know that I am God."[262] The bounds of Zion's enemies "are set, they cannot pass . . . therefore, fear not what man can do, for God shall be with you forever and ever."[263]

---

257 Nibley, *Approaching Zion*, 32–33.
258 D&C 45:66–67, 70.
259 1 Nephi 22:14; see also 2 Nephi 27:3; Moses 7:20.
260 D&C 71:9–11.
261 2 Nephi 14:5.
262 D&C 101:16.
263 D&C 122:9.

Obtaining an Abundance in All Things

Zion exists "that every man may improve upon his talent, that every man may gain other talents, yea, even an hundred fold."[264] Abundance, not poverty, describes Zion. But, as with other principles, abundance and prosperity can be obtained in telestial, terrestrial, and celestial ways and amounts. Motivation for obtaining abundance lies at the heart of the issue. Whereas a telestial wealth is often obtained through hoarding, personal genius, and self-serving efforts, celestial wealth is obtained by obedience to God's commandments, building up his kingdom, and improving the condition of his children.

The telestial and celestial motivations and methods for obtaining and managing abundance are set forth in the scriptures.[265] Nephi stated the frightening situation of telestially gotten wealth: "But wo unto the rich, who are rich as to the things of the world. For because they are rich they despise the poor, and they persecute the meek, and their hearts are upon their treasures; wherefore, their treasure is their God. And behold, their treasure shall perish with them also."[266]

Often, if a man is to become rich, he decides, early in his career, to suppress the urge to take care of his neighbor. He might soothe his conscience by dealing out comfortable portions so that he can look himself in the mirror and declare that he has fulfilled his duty to God and his neighbors. Nevertheless, in the daily management of his affairs, he is ever vigilant to take care to not overstep the bounds of proper business practice. In the eyes of God, however, at the moment that the rich man sets his heart on building his treasure, that man begins to despise the poor and persecute the meek.

On the other hand, Jacob reminded his people of the celestial law of wealth and its motivation: "Think of your brethren like unto yourselves, and be familiar with all and free with your substance, that they may be rich like unto you. But before ye seek for riches, seek ye for the kingdom of God. And after ye have obtained a hope in Christ ye shall obtain riches, if ye seek them; and ye will seek them for the intent to do good—to clothe the naked, and to feed the hungry, and to liberate the captive, and administer relief to the sick and the afflicted."[267] Clearly, celestially-gotten wealth follows those who "seek . . . first the kingdom of God, and his righteousness; *and all these things shall be added unto you.*"[268]

There is an important distinction here between the methods of Babylon and Zion for obtaining wealth. As we are told by substantially every prophet in the Book of Mormon, celestial wealth follows obedience to the commandments of God.[269] Few other commandments are repeated as often as to not seek for riches but rather for the kingdom of God. Some people rationalize their seeking first for riches with the eventual intent of blessing the kingdom of God. But their motive is transparent, and they cannot point to an instance in which God has authorized the sequence.

---

264 D&C 82:19.
265 Alma 30:12–18.
266 2 Nephi 9:30.
267 Jacob 2:17–19.
268 Matthew 6:33.
269 1 Nephi 4:14.

The kingdom must be our first, entire, and eternal focus. We are under covenant now, not later, to use all our time, talents, and means to do God's work, which is to elevate his children.[270] By doing so, God—not Babylon—will subsequently prosper us so that our capacity to bless others will increase and thereby we will be able to give more. In other words, Zion people become a conduit through which God funnels blessings to his children. This is an essential lesson Zion people must incorporate in their lives: We were sent to earth to learn to become like God, who is the most generous *Giver*.

Developing the attitude of selfless giving is a major step we take to remove ourselves from Babylon. We must take this step in order to become Zionlike, for it is impossible to simultaneously serve God and mammon.[271] One master or the other will eventually claim our loyalty. President Stephen L Richards said, "The accumulation and utilization of wealth confront the human family with some of its major challenges in determining the righteousness of goals and the correctness of behavior." Then, quoting Franklin D. Richards, he added, "'In many respects the real test of a man is his attitude toward his earthly possessions' (F. Richards, p. 46). The prosperity that results from honest and intelligent work is not necessarily repugnant to the spiritual quality of life, but the Church consistently warns of the risks of selfishness and personal aggrandizementthat lurk in accumulating wealth (S. Richards, CR [Apr. 1928, 31])."[272] President Richards went on to say that Zion people believe that "everything rightly belongs to God (Mosiah 2:21–25) and comes to man 'in the form of trust property' to be used for God's purposes (S. Richards, CR [Apr. 1923, 151])."[273]

Zion-like abundance and prosperity pivot on the principle of personal righteousness: "Inasmuch as ye shall keep the commandments of God ye shall prosper in the land."[274] In addition, President N. Eldon Tanner outlined five principles for personal economic affairs: "pay an honest tithing, live on less than you earn, distinguish between needs and wants, develop and live within a budget, and be honest in all financial affairs (*Ensign* . . . [Nov. 1979, 81–82])."[275] Consider the payment of tithes and offerings. Has anyone ever been impoverished by paying them? It would be impossible. The true Paymaster invites us to prove, or test, him on this matter, and he will not fail us; he is a God of truth who cannot lie. Millions of tithe payers can attest that the windows of heaven most certainly will burst and pour out blessings that will challenge our ability to receive. Interestingly, it is upon the principle of tithing that we initiate our retreat from Babylon and our return to Zion: "Wherein shall we return? . . . In tithes and offerings." Is it not interesting that tithing saves us from the devourer, ensures that the conditions of a telestial world will not destroy us, and makes of us a blessed and delightsome people?[276] Zion indeed!

---

270 Moses 1:39.
271 Matthew 5:20; 6:24.
272 *Encyclopedia of Mormonism*, s.v. "Wealth, Attitude toward," 1552.
273 *Encyclopedia of Mormonism*, s.v. "Wealth, Attitude toward," 1552.
274 Alma 36:30.
275 *Encyclopedia of Mormonism*, s.v. "Wealth, Attitude toward," 1552.
276 Malachi 3:7–12.

Zion is described as being exceedingly prosperous,[277] which leads us to believe that telestial prosperity, as much as we are awed by it, does not compare to the prosperity enjoyed by Zion people. Of course, the greatest wealth is not to be measured in terms of money: "Remember the worth of souls is great in the sight of God."[278] The Lord added, "And if a person gains more knowledge and intelligence in this life through his diligence and obedience than another, he will have so much the advantage in the world to come."[279] The Lord also counseled, "Lay up for yourselves treasures in heaven."[280] And in our day, "Seek not for riches but for wisdom, and behold, the mysteries of God shall be unfolded unto you, and then shall you be made rich. Behold, he that hath eternal life is rich."[281] Friends, family, wisdom, other celestial characteristics, and eternal life are true wealth.

---

[277] 4 Nephi 1:7.
[278] D&C 18:10.
[279] D&C 130:19.
[280] Matthew 6:20.
[281] D&C 6:7.

Embracing the Law of Consecration

To consecrate something is to sanctify, purify, and set it apart for a sacred use, to make it holy, to dedicate it solemnly to a special service, or to give it religious sanction as with an oath or a vow.[282] When we make the covenant of consecration, we agree to consecrate our lives, including everything that we have, will have, are, or will be. That is, we consecrate "our time, talents and means to care for those in need—whether spiritually or temporally—and in building the Lord's kingdom."[283] Hugh Nibley asked, "And how much is one able to give? Exactly as much as the Lord has given him—all that which the Lord has blessed you, or with which he will bless you."[284] Lived properly, the covenant of consecration paves the way and lays the foundation for the establishment for Zion in a righteous person's life.

One of the first recorded revelations concerning consecration was received on April 7, 1829, when the Lord instructed Joseph Smith to "seek to bring forth and establish the cause of Zion."[285] This was no small task. Zion is the celestial order of things, for both individuals and societies.[286] Some descriptions of consecrated Zion people include:

- Their belief that all things belong to God and that they are stewards[287]
- Their willingness to be unified by esteeming others as themselves[288]
- Their retaining and exercising their free agency[289]
- Their willingness to set aside selfishness and become equal with all the Saints of God, according to their wants, needs, and family situations[290] by consecrating their "time, talents, strength, properties, and monies"[291]
- Their being accountable to the Lord for the discharge of their covenants and stewardships[292]

Anciently, Enoch managed to establish the ideal of Zion among his people, who later joined to create Zion, the city. These people exercised faith in Jesus Christ, repented of their sins, embraced the fullness of the new and everlasting covenant, and thereby became "of one heart and one mind, and dwelt in righteousness; and there was no poor among them."[293] The vehicle that made this condition possible and that will make it possible in the latter-days, was the law of consecration.

At the beginning of 1831, "the Lord revealed to the Prophet Joseph Smith in Fayette, New York, that anciently he had taken the Zion of Enoch to himself and then

---

282 *American Heritage Dictionary*, s.v. "Consecrate" and "Sanctify"
283 Kimball, *The Teachings of Spencer W. Kimball*, 366.
284 Nibley, *Approaching Zion*, 427.
285 D&C 6:6.
286 D&C 105:5.
287 D&C 38:17; 104:11–14.
288 D&C 38:24–27; 51:3, 9; 70:14; 78:6; 82:17.
289 D&C 104:17.
290 D&C 51:3.
291 McConkie, *Mormon Doctrine*, "Consecration,"157.
292 D&C 72:3; 104:13–18.
293 Moses 7:18.

commanded him to go to Ohio to receive the law [the law of Zion]."[294] A month later, on February 9, 1831, the Lord revealed to the Prophet "the law," or the law of Zion, that which the Prophet specified as "embracing the law of the Church."[295] This law became known as section 42 of the Doctrine and Covenants, and in it the Lord revealed the cornerstones of the law of consecration[296]:

- First, mutual assistance—the Lord expects his disciples to sustain and help one another.
- Second, proper use of priesthood—the priesthood is to be used to benefit those who are physically and spiritually ill or in need.
- Third, the need for faith—according to God's will, a person can be healed [physically, emotionally, and spiritually] by the power of the priesthood if that individual has faith in Jesus Christ and if he is "not appointed unto death," information that gives confidence to the person as he realizes that the Lord has given him time to work out his exaltation.
- Fourth, reciprocal love—the Lord expects his disciples to love one another and to become one.

President Ezra Taft Benson said, "The law of consecration is a law for an inheritance in the celestial kingdom. God, the Eternal Father, His Son Jesus Christ, and all holy beings abide by this law. It is an eternal law."[297] People whose lives are consecrated to the Lord "set their hearts on righteousness and having actually put first in their lives the things of God's kingdom."[298]

The Church welfare plan describes a consecrated person as one who does not seek for worldly riches; who esteems his brother as himself; who, through tithes and offerings, helps to build up the kingdom of God by caring for the temporal needs of those General Authorities whom God has called into full-time service; who makes his worldly goods available, over and above his family's necessities, for the Lord's work; and who, with his time, talents, and means, takes care of the temporally and spiritually poor.[299]

Quoting the Church welfare plan, Elder Bruce R. McConkie wrote, "The practice of the law of consecration is inextricably intertwined with the development of the attributes of godliness in this life and the attainment of eternal life in the world to come. 'The law pertaining to material aid is so formulated that the carrying of it out necessitates practices calculated to root out human traits not in harmony with requirements for living in the celestial kingdom and replacing those inharmonious traits with the virtues and character essential to life in that abode.' (Bowen, *The Church Welfare Plan*, p. 13)."[300] Then, quoting a supporting scripture, Elder McConkie added, "For if you will that I give you a

---

294 *Encyclopedia of Mormonism*, s.v. "Consecration," 312.
295 D&C 42, Introduction.
296 List adapted from Clark V. Johnson, Sperry Symposium 1989, "The Law of consecration: The Covenant That Requires All and Gives Everything."
297 Benson, *The Teachings of Ezra Taft Benson*, 121.
298 McConkie, *Mormon Doctrine*, "Consecration," 157.
299 Bowen, *The Church Welfare Plan*, 6.
300 McConkie, *Mormon Doctrine*, "Consecration," 157.

place in the celestial world, you must prepare yourselves by doing the things which I have commanded you and required of you."[301]

Elsewhere in the scriptures, we learn that the law of consecration is built on the foundational principles of agency, stewardship, accountability, and labor.

Agency

An agent is someone who has the power and authority to act.[302] Therefore, agents have agency, which is the ability to "act for themselves,"[303] or the ability to act for themselves with respect to a given responsibility or obligation.[304] Agents have the capacity to be accountable for their actions. Whereas *freedom* is the power and privilege to exercise our will and act upon it, *agency* is the power, independence of mind, and individual will to choose in the first place.

Elder McConkie wrote: "Four great principles must be in force if there is to be agency: 1. Laws must exist, laws ordained by an Omnipotent power, laws which can be obeyed or disobeyed; 2. Opposites must exist—good and evil, virtue and vice, right and wrong—that is, there must be an opposition, one force pulling one way and another pulling the other; 3. A knowledge of good and evil must be had by those who are to enjoy the agency, that is, they must know the difference between the opposites; and 4. An unfettered power of choice must prevail."[305]

Moral agency describes our ability to act upon and be accountable for spiritual matters.[306] Zion people exercise their God-given agency to choose to make and keep covenants and to reject the enticements of Babylon. And choose we must. Posing the choice between Zion and Babylon, Elijah asked, "How long halt ye between two opinions? if the Lord be God, follow him: but if Baal [Babylon], then follow him."[307] Being lukewarm on the issue is not acceptable: "I know thy works, that thou art neither cold nor hot: I would thou wert cold or hot. So then because thou art lukewarm, and neither cold nor hot, I will spue thee out of my mouth."[308]

That opposites exist makes agency possible: "And it must needs be that the devil should tempt the children of men, or they could not be agents unto themselves; for if they never should have bitter they could not know the sweet."[309] Therefore, we are free to choose our destiny: Zion, to our salvation, or Babylon, to our condemnation. "Behold, here is the agency of man, and here is the condemnation of man; because that which was from the beginning is plainly manifest unto them, and they receive not the light."[310] Having chosen Zion and thus having overcome Babylon, Zion people enjoy the highest degree of moral agency and its resulting freedom.

---

301 D&C 78:7.
302 See *American Heritage Dictionary*, s.v. "Agent"
303 2 Nephi 2:26.
304 D&C 29:35.
305 McConkie, *Mormon Doctrine*, "Agency," 26.
306 D&C 29:35.
307 1 Kings 18:21, insertion added.
308 Revelation 3:15–16.
309 D&C 29:39.
310 D&C 93:31.

Agency and freedom flourish in Zion: "If the Son therefore shall make you free, ye shall be free indeed."[311] "And because that they are redeemed from the fall they have become free forever, knowing good from evil; to act for themselves and not to be acted upon."[312]

Agency and freedom decrease in Babylon: "And the whole world [Babylon] lieth in sin, and groaneth under darkness and under the bondage of sin."[313] Choosing Babylon results in fewer choices and less freedom to exercise agency, while choosing Zion results in limitless choices and unequalled freedom to exercise agency.

Stewardship

When a person exercises his agency to abide in the Covenant, he makes a conscious choice to become a steward of the Lord's property. His approach to ownership is "the earth is the Lord's, and the fulness thereof."[314] Elder Bruce R. McConkie said, "Underlying this principle of stewardship is the eternal gospel truth that all things belong to the Lord. 'I, the Lord, stretched out the heavens, and built the earth, my very handiwork; and all things therein are mine. . . . Behold, all these properties are mine. . . . And if the properties are mine, then ye are stewards; otherwise ye are no stewards.' (D&C 104:14, 55–56)."[315]

We are expressly forbidden to hoard property or claim it as our own: "I command thee that thou shalt not covet thine own property."[316] Therefore, a Zion person's claim to his property is subordinate to the Lord's claim. As Martin Harris learned, property must be consecrated for the building up of the kingdom of God and the establishment of Zion, which provides that no poor should exist among us. Ultimately we will be held accountable for the discharge of our stewardship.[317]

A Zion person's stewardship is sometimes referred to as "portion,"[318] or "inheritance."[319] It is to be used to support his own family, and then "conveying back to the Lord's storehouse any surplus which accrued [for the poor]. (D&C 42:33–34, 55; 70:7–10)." Elder McConkie added, "It is by the wise use of one's stewardship that eternal life is won."[320]

Zion people do not take their covenant of stewardship lightly; they know that everything depends on their faithfulness in this responsibility: "And whoso is found a faithful, a just, and a wise steward shall enter into the joy of his Lord, and shall inherit eternal life."[321]

---

311 John 8:36.
312 2 Nephi 2:26.
313 D&C 84:49–50.
314 Psalms 24:1.
315 McConkie, *Mormon Doctrine*, "Stewardships," 767.
316 D&C 19:26.
317 D&C 72:3–4; 51:19; Matthew 25:14–30; Luke 16:2; 19:17; D&C 82:3, 11; 78:22.
318 D&C 51:4.
319 D&C 51:4; 57:15.
320 McConkie, *Mormon Doctrine*, "Stewardships," 767.
321 D&C 51:19.

Accountability

The Lord said, "Every man shall be made accountable unto me, a steward over his own property."[322] Upon the principle of moral agency, stewards are free to manage their stewardships, but they are not free from being accountable to the Lord: "It is required of the Lord, at the hand of every steward, to render an account of his stewardship, both in time and in eternity. For he who is faithful and wise in time is accounted worthy to inherit the mansions prepared for him of my Father."[323] Clearly, we will one day stand before God to give an accounting of our deeds, which will include the management of our stewardships. Our performance will determine the trusts and stewardships given to us in eternity.

Zion people are under covenant to account for their earthly stewardships to the Lord's servant, the bishop: "Verily I say unto you, the elders of the church in this part of my vineyard shall render an account of their stewardship unto the bishop, who shall be appointed of me in this part of my vineyard. These things shall be had on record, to be handed over unto the bishop in Zion."[324] For this reason, we report to the bishop each year regarding our tithes and offerings.

Labor

Elder Bruce R. McConkie wrote, "Work is the great basic principle which makes all things possible both in time and in eternity. Men, spirits, angels, and Gods use their physical and mental powers in work."[325]

Work, like other gospel principles, exists in degrees ranging from telestial to celestial. Adam was commanded to work in this telestial world to support his family.[326] Because of his approach to work, his was a celestial endeavor. We note with interest that he was not commanded to set his sights on empire building, plundering, extorting, leveraging, competing, augmenting his balance sheet, or amassing personal wealth on the backs of the poor, all of which are telestial.

Adam worked to create the first Zion upon the earth: Adam-ondi-Ahman. There he labored to sustain his immediate family and to bless the lives of others. Likewise, Enoch worked to establish Zion, as did Melchizedek and Nephi: "And it came to pass that I, Nephi, did cause my people to be industrious, and to labor with their hands."[327] Nephi's Zion-like people worked together for the benefit of all. They labored to establish righteousness. They worked in unity to raise crops, smelt ore to create weapons for defense, and fashion objects of beauty. They built buildings and a temple. Because of their celestial level of labor they were blessed with prosperity and familial strength: "And it came to pass that we began to prosper exceedingly, and to multiply in the land."[328]

---

322 D&C 42:32.
323 D&C 72:3–4.
324 D&C 72:5–6.
325 McConkie, *Mormon Doctrine*, "Work," 847.
326 Genesis 3:19.
327 2 Nephi 5:17.
328 2 Ne 5:10–16.

Things began to fall apart when the Nephites became selfish and began to work on a telestial level. Jacob chastised his people for searching "for gold, and for silver, and for all manner of precious ores." They were doing these things for the purpose of obtaining riches "more abundantly than that of [their] brethren," causing the errant ones to be "lifted up in the pride of [their] hearts," and supposing that they were better than others.[329] This kind of labor is not justified in Zion; it is condemned. President Kimball said, "As I understand these matters, Zion can be established only by those who are pure in heart, and who labor for Zion, for the 'laborer in Zion shall labor for Zion; for if they labor for money [riches] they shall perish.'"[330]

Jacob taught his people the celestial law of labor and its underlying motivation: "Think of your brethren like unto yourselves, and be familiar with all and free with your substance, that they may be rich like unto you. But before ye seek for riches, seek ye for the kingdom of God. And after ye have obtained a hope in Christ ye shall obtain riches, if ye seek them; and ye will seek them for the intent to do good—to clothe the naked, and to feed the hungry, and to liberate the captive, and administer relief to the sick and the afflicted."[331]

Clearly, we must work, but what we work for determines if the work is telestial or celestial. Conversely, "idleness has no place [in Zion]," said President Benson, "and greed, selfishness, and covetousness are condemned. [Zion] may therefore operate only with a righteous people."[332]

These four principles—agency, stewardship, accountability, and labor—form the foundation of the law of consecration, which is the law a person must keep if he hopes to become pure in heart in this life and qualify for eternal life in the world to come. Only upon the principle of consecration is the kingdom of God built up and Zion established as an individual, family, ward, stake, or Church.

---

329 Jacob 2:12–14.
330 Kimball, "Becoming the Pure in Heart."
331 Jacob 2:17–19.
332 Benson, "A Vision and a Hope for the Youth of Zion," *Devotional Speeches of the Year*, 74.

Enjoying God's Presence

Zion is the habitation of the Lord.[333] A Zion person harbors the hope that one day the Father and the Son will make their abode with him. This is one of the primary reasons—to enjoy God's presence—a person enters into the new and everlasting covenant. To enjoy God's presence is the promised result and the supernal blessing for abiding in the Covenant. Joseph Smith said,

> "If a man love me, he will keep my word: and my Father will love him, and *we will come unto him, and make our abode with him.*" Now what is this other Comforter? It is no more nor less than the Lord Jesus Christ Himself; and this is the sum and substance of the whole matter; that when any man obtains this last Comforter, he will have the personage of Jesus Christ to attend him, or appear unto him from time to time, and even He will manifest the Father unto him, *and they will take up their abode with him,* and the visions of the heavens will be opened unto him, and the Lord will teach him face to face, and he may have a perfect knowledge of the mysteries of the Kingdom of God; and this is the state and place the ancient Saints arrived at when they had such glorious visions—Isaiah, Ezekiel, John upon the Isle of Patmos, St. Paul in the three heavens, and all the Saints who held communion with the general assembly and Church of the Firstborn.[334]

The scriptures state, "They who dwell in [God's] presence are the church of the Firstborn."[335] Interestingly, the Church of the Firstborn is also synonymous with the Church of Enoch,[336] or the "Order of Enoch,"[337] which is synonymous with Zion. The Book of Mormon refers to the Church of the Firstborn as the "rest of the Lord," meaning the "fulness of his glory."[338] Speaking of this heavenly church, Elder McConkie wrote, "This is the Church which exists among exalted beings in the celestial realm. But it has its beginning here on earth. Members of The Church of Jesus Christ of Latter-day Saints who so devote themselves to righteousness that they receive the higher ordinances of exaltation become members of the Church of the Firstborn. Baptism is the gate to the Church itself, but celestial marriage is the gate to membership in the Church of the First-

---

333 Psalms 132:13; Moses 7:21; see also Psalms 9:11; 76:2; Isaiah 24:23; 59:20; 60:14; Jeremiah 8:19; Joel 3:16; Micah 4:7; D&C 97:19; 105:32.
334 Smith, *Teachings of the Prophet Joseph Smith,* 150; emphasis added.
335 D&C 76:94.
336 D&C 76:67.
337 Young, *Discourses of Brigham Young,* 179.
338 D&C 84:17–24; see Alma 13:11–12.

born, the inner circle of faithful saints who are heirs of exaltation and the fulness of the Father's kingdom. (D&C 76:54, 67, 71, 94, 102; 77:11; 78:21; 88:1–5; Heb. 12:23)."[339]

Continuing, he said, "Those who attain this state of cleanliness and perfection are able, as occasion may require, to see God and view the things of his kingdom. (D&C 84:23; 88:68; Ether 4:7).[340] Indeed, the ultimate privileges of God's holy authority are spoken of as follows: 'The power and authority of the higher, or Melchizedek Priesthood, is to hold the keys of all the spiritual blessings of the church—to have the privilege of receiving the mysteries of the kingdom of heaven, to have the heavens opened unto them, to commune with the general assembly and church of the Firstborn, and to enjoy the communion and presence of God the Father, and Jesus the mediator of the new covenant' (D&C 107:18–19)."[341]

"While in the flesh," Zion people can qualify for the "privilege of seeing and knowing for themselves."[342] The Father and the Son will come and make their abode with them, as the Prophet Joseph Smith said, and because they have made their hearts pure by abiding the Covenant, "they shall see God."[343]

---

[339] McConkie, *Doctrinal New Testament Commentary*, 3:231.
[340] McConkie, *Mormon Doctrine*, 2d ed., "Sanctification," 675.
[341] McConkie, *Doctrinal New Testament Commentary*, 3:231.
[342] D&C 76:117.
[343] JST, Matthew 5:10; 3 Nephi 12:8.

Conclusion

This, then, is a portrait of a Zion person, the ideal to which we all should aspire. We may not achieve the ultimate expression of perfection of Zion in this life, but we must "relentlessly chase perfection," as Vince Lombardi is quoted as saying, "knowing full well we will not catch it, but . . . in the process we will catch excellence."[344] This portrait of a Zion person contains no new revelation. Joseph Smith, whose mission it was to restore the fullness of the gospel, received every revelation, covenant, and power regarding the establishment of Zion. Therefore, we have everything we need to become individually pure in heart and Zion-like. The law of Zion is not in our future; we have the law, and we are expected to live it *now*. We have made the Covenant; we simply need to embrace it. Everything of eternal consequence hinges on our obedience and diligence living this law.

Prefacing the eternal law of marriage, which is the crowning order of the new and everlasting covenant and the gate to Zion,[345] the Lord revealed the following essential information regarding the Covenant:

> Prepare thy heart to receive and obey the instructions which I am about to give unto you; *for all those who have this law revealed unto them must obey the same.* For behold, I reveal unto you a new and an everlasting covenant; *and if ye abide not that covenant, then are ye damned; for no one can reject this covenant and be permitted to enter into my glory.* For all who will have a blessing at my hands shall abide the law which was appointed for that blessing, and the conditions thereof, as were instituted from before the foundation of the world. And as pertaining to the new and everlasting covenant, *it was instituted for the fulness of my glory; and he that receiveth a fulness thereof must and shall abide the law, or he shall be damned, saith the Lord God.*[346]

In vision, Nephi saw the latter-day members of the Church who had made the Covenant. To his dismay, he saw widespread apathy; we had neglected the Covenant in favor of carnal security. We had been lulled away from the Covenant by Satan, and we were ignorantly under the impression that "All is well in Zion; yea, Zion prospereth, all is well."[347]

While it is true that all is well with the Church, it is not necessarily "well" with many of its members. Nephi saw that our carnal appetites had allowed the devil to "cheat our souls" with the purpose of "leading us away carefully down to hell."[348] According to Brigham Young, carnal security, materialism, and wealth seeking are the devil's clever "decoys" that

---

344   Jeremy Schaap, *Parade Magazine*, "We Will Catch Excellence," February 3, 2008.
345   McConkie, *Doctrinal New Testament Commentary*, 3:231.
346   D&C 132:3–6, emphasis added.
347   2 Nephi 28:21.
348   2 Nephi 28:21.

drive a wedge between Zion and us. The metaphor is chilling. A decoy is something that looks like the real thing but is meant to trap its victim. A decoy is cleverly disguised, but it is deadly if you get too close to it. President Young said, "It is a fearful deception which all the world labors under, *and many of this people too, who profess to be not of the world,* that gold is wealth."[349] The only solution is the one Nephi offered when confronted by the people in the great and spacious building: "We heeded them not."[350] That is, "we did not allow ourselves to become distracted. We were determined to abide in the Covenant regardless of what Babylon said or offered us." Only abiding in the Covenant provides real security.

Of course, this is a tall order. You might ask, "What will become of me if I attempt to step away from Babylon and fully embrace the principles of Zion?" The answer is always the same: "Seek ye first the kingdom of God and his righteousness, and all these things shall be added unto you."[351] The solution is imbedded in the Covenant; it is God's promise. He will support us, sustain us, stand beside us, and keep us safe: "Surely Zion shall dwell in safety forever."[352] Safe in the Covenant, we no longer have to worry like we did in Babylon: "Therefore take no thought, saying, What shall we eat? or, What shall we drink? or, Wherewithal shall we be clothed? For your heavenly Father knoweth that ye have need of all these things."[353] This takes faith, lots of faith. Consequently, no one can come to Zion alone. Only the Atonement of Jesus Christ can make the journey possible. The Atonement has the power to purify our hearts, make of us celestial people, secure for us a celestial resurrection, make us heirs of God's kingdom, and bind to us our spouse and family forever.

The subject of Zion permeates prophetic teaching: "The prophets always labor to prepare people to become a people of Zion. Sometimes people embrace Zion; most often they do not."[354] Why would we choose to reject the principles of Zion? Perhaps because of fear. We might say to ourselves, "Zion and consecration are well and good, but I don't want to be the first to live them. Therefore, I will wait for the president of the Church to reveal a program." This is a dangerous attitude fraught with folly. As we have previously asked: "Which of our covenants, having been made, is waiting for a program from Church headquarters? Baptism? Sabbath-day observance? Temple worship? Eternal marriage? Why, then, do we consider parts of the new and everlasting covenant, especially consecration, to be futuristic? We know the principles of Zion, so what stops us from living them? Clearly, Babylon has a hold on us that we fear to break. But if we would consider the payment of tithes and offerings as an indication of Zion's safety and prosperity, then we might, with confidence, press through our fear and embrace Zion in its entirety, as we have covenanted to do. Perhaps to that end the Lord encourages us to consider the lilies of the field.[355] Most certainly, he will take care of his covenant people. The Book of Mormon is a textbook on the subject."

During the ministry of Christ, a fierce storm arose, threatening to capsize the Apostles' boat. Panicked, they awakened the Savior and cried, "Master, carest thou not that we perish?

---

349 Young, *Journal of Discourses*, 10:271, emphasis added.
350 1 Nephi 8:33.
351 Matthew 6:33; 3 Nephi 13:33.
352 Moses 7:20.
353 3 Nephi 13:31–32.
354 *Encyclopedia of Mormonism*, s.v. "Zion," 1625.
355 Matthew 6:28–29; 3 Nephi 13:28–29.

Introduction   Portrait of a Zion Person   **43**

And he arose, rebuked the wind, and said unto the sea, Peace, be still. And the wind ceased, and there was a great calm. And he said unto them, Why are ye so fearful? how is it that ye have no faith?"[356] In other words, "Why were you afraid knowing that I was with you? Where is your faith?" As we have learned, wherever Zion is, there is the Lord. If he is with us, and we know that he commanded us to live the new and everlasting covenant, to strive to build up the kingdom of God, to seek the establishment of Zion, and to believe that he will stand beside us, what have we to fear? We will not be disappointed. We, like the Nephites, will experience for ourselves the safety, abundance, and joy of Zion, for "surely there could not be a happier people among all the people who had been created by the hand of God."[357]

Finally, if we intend to become Zion people, we must change the paradigm of our belief. In too many instances, we do not believe what our faith tells us. Often, we believe in a convenient gospel with the expectation that God, if he wants to, will move us along and eventually reward us with extraordinary blessings in the end. But Zion cannot be established either in an individual's life, a marriage, a family, or in a priesthood society on such a philosophy. Zion has always been established by people believing *all* that their faith teaches them.

If we truly want to become Zion people, we must believe what our faith tells us about Zion. Zion is the pure in heart, those who ultimately qualify to see God. Will that happen without invoking the law of seeking Zion and asking the Lord to make of us that kind of person? Of course not. No blessings arrive unbidden. We must work for them. "Verily, thus saith the Lord: It shall come to pass that every soul who forsaketh his sins and cometh unto me, and calleth on my name, and obeyeth my voice, and keepeth my commandments, shall see my face and know that I am."[358]

This, then, is a portrait of a Zion person. By becoming such a person, we hope to achieve that which the 3 Nephi saints achieved.

> And it came to pass that there was no contention in the land, because of the love of God which did dwell in the hearts of the people.
>
> And there were no envyings, nor strifes, nor tumults, nor whoredoms, nor lyings, nor murders, nor any manner of lasciviousness; and surely there could not be a happier people among all the people who had been created by the hand of God.
>
> There were no robbers, nor murderers, neither were there Lamanites, nor any manner of -ites; but they were in one, the children of Christ, and heirs to the kingdom of God.
>
> And how blessed were they! For the Lord did bless them in all their doings.[359]

---

356   Mark 4:38–40.
357   4 Nephi 1:16.
358   D&C 93:1.
359   4 Nephi 1:15–18.

Bibliography

American Heritage Dictionary. Boston, MA: Houghton Mifflin, 2000.

Anderson, Dawn Hall, Susette Fletcher Green, and Dlora Hall Dalton, eds. *Clothed with Charity: Talks from the 1996 Women's Conference.* Salt Lake City, UT: Deseret Book, 1997.

Asay, Carlos E. "The Oath and Covenant of the Priesthood," *Ensign*, November 1985.

—*Family Pecan Trees: Planting a Legacy of Faith at Home.* Salt Lake City, UT: Deseret Book, 1992.

—*The Seven M's of Missionary Service: Proclaiming the Gospel as a Member or Full-time Missionary.* Salt Lake City, UT: Bookcraft, 1996.

Ashton, Marvin J. "Be a Quality Person," *Ensign*, February 1993.

—"Love Takes Time," *Ensign*, November 1975.

Bednar, David A. "Pray Always," *Ensign*, November 2008.

Benson, Ezra Taft. "A Vision and a Hope for the Youth of Zion," *Devotional Speeches of the Year*. Provo, UT: Brigham Young University Press, 1978.

—*A Witness and a Warning: A Modern-Day Prophet Testifies of the Book of Mormon.* Salt Lake City, UT: Deseret Book, 1988.

—"Beware of Pride," *Ensign*, May 1989.

—*Devotional Speeches of the Year.* Provo, UT: Brigham Young University Press, 1978.

—*God, Family, Country: Our Three Great Loyalties.* Salt Lake City, UT: Deseret Book, 1975.

—"In His Steps," *Ensign*, September 1988.

—"Jesus Christ—Gifts and Expectations," *New Era*, May 1975.

—*The Teachings of Ezra Taft Benson.* Salt Lake City, UT: Deseret Book, 1988.

—"What I Hope You Will Teach Your Children about the Temple," *Ensign*, August 1985;

Bible Dictionary. Salt Lake City, UT: The Church of Jesus Christ of Latter-day Saints, 1989;

Black, Susan Easton, et al. *Doctrines for Exaltation: The 1989 Sperry Symposium on the Doctrine and Covenants.* Salt Lake City, UT: Deseret Book, *1989*.

—*The Iowa Mormon Trail: Legacy of Faith and Courage.* Orem, UT: Helix Publishing, 1997.

Bowen, Albert E. *The Church Welfare Plan.* Salt Lake City, UT: The Church of Jesus Christ of Latter-day Saints, 1946.

Brewster, Hoyt W. Jr. *Doctrine and Covenants Encyclopedia.* Salt Lake City, UT: Bookcraft, 1988.

Brown, Hugh B. *Continuing the Quest.* Salt Lake City, UT: Bookcraft, 1961.

Brown, Matthew B. *Prophecies: The Gate of Heaven.* American Fork, UT: Covenant Communications, 1999.

—*Signs of the Times, Second Coming, Millennium.* American Fork, UT: Covenant Communications, 2006.

Budge, Ernest A. Wallis. *Coptic Martyrdoms Discourse on Abbaton.* London: British Museum, 1914.

Burton, Alma P., ed. *Discourses of the Prophet Joseph Smith.* Salt Lake City, UT: Deseret Book, 1956.

Cannon, Donald Q. *Teachings of the Latter-day Prophets.* Salt Lake City, UT: Bookcraft, 1998.

Cannon, Elaine. "Agency and Accountability." Salt Lake City, *Ensign*, November 1983.

Bibliography

Cannon, George Q. "Beware Lest Ye Fall." Discourse delivered at the Morgan Utah Stake Conference, Sunday, February 16, 1896.

—*Gospel Truth: Discourses and Writings of President George Q. Cannon.* Salt Lake City, UT: Deseret Book, 1974.

Cannon, Joseph A. "Sanctification," *Mormon Times,* June 12, 2008, http://www.mormontimes.com.

Clark, E. Douglas. *The Blessings of Abraham—Becoming a Zion People.* American Fork, UT: Covenant Communications, 2005.

Clark, J. Reuben. *Church Welfare Plan: A Discussion.* Salt Lake, City, UT General Church Welfare Committee, 1939.

Clark, James R., comp., *Messages of the First Presidency of The Church of Jesus Christ of Latter-day Saints.* Salt Lake City: Bookcraft, 1965–75.

Clarke, Adam. *Clarke's Commentary on the Bible.* Grand Rapids, MI: Baker Book House, 1967.

Clarke, J. Richard. "Successful Welfare Stewardship," *Ensign,* November 1978.

Conference Report, 1897–2009, Salt Lake City, UT: The Church of Jesus Christ of Latter-day Saints.

Cook, Gene R. "Home and Family: A Divine Eternal Pattern," *Ensign,* May 1984.

—"The Seat Next to You," *New Era,* October 1983.

Cook, Lyndon. *Joseph Smith and the Law of Consecration.* Provo, UT: Keepsake Books, 1991.

Cowley, Matthew. *Matthew Cowley Speaks: Discourses of Elder Matthew Cowley of the Quorum of the Twelve of the Church of Jesus Christ of Latter-day Saints.* Salt Lake City, UT: Deseret Book Company, 1954.

Dalrymple, G. Brent. *The Age of the Earth.* Stanford, CA: Stanford University Press, 1991.

Dellenbach, Robert K. "Hour of Conversion," *New Era,* June 2002.

DeMille, Cecil B. *BYU Speeches of the Year.* Provo, UT: Brigham Young University Press, May 1957.

Durham, G. Homer, ed. *The Gospel Kingdom: Selections from the Writings and Discourses of John Taylor, Third President of The Church of Jesus Christ of Latter-day Saints.* Salt Lake City, UT: Bookcraft, 1943.

—*Gospel Ideals: Selections from the Discourses of David O. McKay.* Salt Lake City, UT: Improvement Era, 1953.

Dibble, Philo. "Recollections of the Prophet Joseph Smith," *Juvenile Instructor,* June 1892.

Duffin, James G. "A Character Test," *Improvement Era,* February 1911.

Easton, M. G. *Illustrated Bible Dictionary.* Nashville: TN: Thomas Nelson, 1897.

"The Bondage of Sin," *Improvement Era,* February 1923.

Ehat, Andrew F. and Lyndon W. Cook. *The Words of Joseph Smith: The Contemporary Accounts of the Nauvoo Discourses of the Prophet Joseph.* Provo, UT: Religious Studies Center Brigham Young University, 1980.

Encarta World English Dictionary. New York, NY: St. Martins Press, 1999.

Eyring, Henry B. "Faith and the Oath and Covenant of the Priesthood," *Ensign,* May 2008.

Farley, S. Brent. "The Oath and Covenant of the Priesthood." *Sperry Symposium on the Doctrine and Covenants.* Salt Lake City: Desert Book, 1989.

First Presidency, "What is the Doctrine of the Priesthood?" Salt Lake City, UT: *Improvement Era,* February 1961.

Faust, James E. "A Royal Priesthood," *Ensign,* May 2006.

—*In the Strength of the Lord: The Life and Teachings of James E. Faust.* Salt Lake City, UT: Deseret Book, 1999.

—"He Healeth the Broken Heart," *Ensign* July 2005.

—"Our Search for Happiness, *Ensign,* Oct. 2000.

—"Standing in Holy Places," *Ensign,* May 2005.

—"The Devil's Throat," *Ensign,* May 2003.

—"The Gift of the Holy Ghost—A Sure Compass," *Ensign,* April 1996.

—"The Shield of Faith," *Ensign,* May 2000.

"Galaxy Map." Washington D.C.: The National Geographic Society, June 1983.

Galbraith, David B., D. Kelly Ogden, and Andrew C. Skinner. *Jerusalem—The Eternal City.* Salt Lake City, UT: Deseret Book, 1996.

Gardner, R. Quinn. "Becoming a Zion Society," *Ensign,* February 1979.

—"I Have a Question," *Ensign,* March 1978.

Gibbons, Ted L. *Be Not Afraid,* Springville, UT: Cedar Fort, Inc., 2009.

Goddard, Wallace H. "Blessed by Angels." *MeridianMagazine.com,* July 27, 2009.

—*Drawing Heaven into Your Marriage.* Fairfax, VA: Meridian Publishing, 2007.

Grant, Heber J. *Teachings of Presidents of the Church.* Salt Lake City, UT: *The Church of Jesus Christ of Latter-day Saints,* 2002.

Guralnik, David B., ed. *Webster's New World Dictionary, 2nd College Edition.* New York City, NY: The New World Publishing Company, 1970.

Hafen, Bruce C. *The Broken Heart: Applying the Atonement to Life's Experiences.* Salt Lake City, UT: Deseret Book, 1989.

Haight, David B. "The Sacrament and the Sacrifice," *Ensign,* November 1989.

Hamilton, Edith. *Spokesman for God.* New York, NY: Norton and Company, 1977.

Hinckley, Gordon B. "Blessed Are the Merciful," *Ensign,* May 1990.

—*Faith: The Essence of True Religion.* Salt Lake City, UT: Deseret Book, 1989.

—"Our Mission of Saving," *Ensign,* November 1991.

—"Priesthood: The Power of Godliness," *Improvement Era,* December 1970.

—*Stand a Little Taller.* Salt Lake City, UT: Eagle Gate, 2000.

—*Standing for Something.* New York, NY: Three Rivers Press, 2000.

—*Teachings of Gordon B. Hinckley.* Salt Lake City, UT: Deseret Book, 2002.

—"The Dawning of a Brighter Day," *Ensign,* May 2004.

—"The Stone Cut Out of the Mountain," *Ensign,* 2007.

—"Till We Meet Again," *Ensign,* November 2001.

—"We Thank Thee for This Sacred Structure," *Church News,* 8 November 1997.

— "Your Greatest Challenge, Mother," *Ensign,* November 2000.

Holland, Jeffrey R. "Broken Things to Mend," *Ensign,* May 2006.

—"However Long and Hard the Road," *Ensign,* September 2002.

—*On Earth As It Is in Heaven.* Salt Lake City, UT: Deseret Book, 1989.

Bibliography

Holzapfel, Richard Neitzel and Thomas A. Wayment, eds., *The Life and Teachings of Jesus Christ: From the Transfiguration through the Triumphant Entry.* Salt Lake City, UT: Deseret Book, 2006.

Horton, George A. "Abraham's Act of Faith Reflects 'a Soul Like Unto Our Savior,'" *LDS Church News,* April 2, 1994.

"'Hymn of the Pearl': an Ancient Counterpart To 'O My Father.'" *BYU Studies,* vol. 36, 1996–97.

Hymns of the Church of Jesus Christ of Latter-day Saints. Salt Lake City, UT: The Church of Jesus Christ of Latter-day Saints, 1985.

Jackson, Kent P. and Robert L. Millet. eds. *Studies in Scripture.* Salt Lake City, UT: Deseret Book 1989.

Jensen, Marlin K. "Living after the Manner of Happiness," *Ensign,* December 2002.

—"An Eye Single to the Glory of God," *Ensign,* Nov. 1989.

Jenson, Andrew, *Historical Record: A Monthly Periodical.* Salt Lake City, UT: Deseret News, 1886—1890.

Jessee, Dean. "Joseph Knight's Recollection of Early Mormon History." Provo, UT: *BYU Studies,* vol. 17, no. 1, 1976.

Johnson, Clark V. *Doctrines for Exaltation: The 1989 Sperry Symposium on the Doctrine and Covenants.* Salt Lake City, UT: Deseret Book, 1989.

Josephus. *Complete Works.* William Whiston, trans., Grand Rapids, MI: Kregal Publications, 1960.

Kimball, Spencer W. "A Gift of Gratitude," *Tambuli,* December 1977.

—"Becoming the Pure in Heart," *Ensign,* May 1978.

—*Faith Precedes the Miracle: Based on Discourses of Spencer W. Kimball.* Salt Lake City, UT: Deseret Book, 1972.

—"The Fruit of Our Welfare Services Labors," *Ensign,* November 1978.

—"The Role of Righteous Women," *Ensign,* November 1979.

—*The Teachings of Spencer W. Kimball.* Salt Lake City, UT: Bookcraft, 1982.

—"Welfare Services: The Gospel in Action," *Ensign,* November 1977.

—"Young Women Fireside 1981—In Love and Power and without Fear," *New Era,* July 1981.

Kirchhoff, Frederick. "Reconstruction of Self in Wordsworth's 'Ode on Intimations of Immortality from Recollections of Early Childhood.'" *Narcissism and the Text.* New York, NY: New York University Press, 1986.

Kirtland Council Minute Book, eds. Fred Collier and William S. Hartwell, Salt Lake City, UT: Collier's Publishing, 1996.

Largey, Dennis L. *Book of Mormon Reference Companion.* Salt Lake City, UT: Deseret Book, 2003.

Larsen, Dean L. "A Royal Generation," *Ensign,* May 1983.

Larson, Stan "The King Follett Discourse: a Newly Amalgamated Text." Provo, UT: *BYU Studies,* Vol. 18, 1977–1978.

Layton, Lynne and Schapiro, Barbara A. *Narcissism and the Text: Studies in Literature and the Psychology of Self.* New York, NY: New York University Press, 1986.

Lee, Harold B. *Decisions for Successful Living.* Salt Lake City, UT: Deseret Book, 1973.
—"Stand Ye in Holy Places," *Ensign,* July 1973.
—*The Teachings of Harold B. Lee.* Salt Lake City, UT: Deseret Book, 1974.
Lightner, Mary. Address to Brigham Young University. *BYU Archives and Manuscripts, Writings of Early Latter-day Saints,* 1905.
Ludlow, Daniel H. *A Companion to Your Study of the Book of Mormon.* Salt Lake City, UT: Deseret Book, 1976.
—*Encyclopedia of Mormonism.* New York City, NY: Macmillan Publishing, 1992.
Lund, Gerald N. *Jesus Christ, Key to the Plan of Salvation.* Salt Lake City, UT: Deseret Book, 1991.
—"Old Testament Types and Symbols," *A Witness of Jesus Christ: The 1989 Sperry Symposium on the Old Testament.* ed. Richard D. Draper, Salt Lake City, UT: Deseret Book, 1990.
Lundquist, John M. and Stephen D. Ricks, eds. *By Study and Also by Faith: Essays in Honor of Hugh W. Nibley on the Occasion of His Eightieth Birthday.* Provo, UT: Maxwell Institute, 1992.
Lundwall, N. B. *Temples of the Most High.* Salt Lake City, UT: Bookcraft, 1965.
"Map: Old Testament Stories: Part Two," *Deseret News.* Jan. 8, 1994.
Maxwell, Cory H., ed. *The Neal A. Maxwell Quote Book.* Salt Lake City, UT: Bookcraft, 1997.
Maxwell, Neal A. *A Wonderful Flood of Light.* Salt Lake City, UT: Deseret Book, 1991.
—*But for a Small Moment.* Salt Lake City, UT: Bookcraft, 1987.
—"Consecrate Thy Performance." *Ensign,* May 2002.
—*Disposition of a Disciple.* Salt Lake City, UT: Deseret Book, 1976.
—"Enduring Well," *Ensign,* April 1997.
—*Even As I Am.* Salt Lake City, UT: Deseret Book, 1991.
—*If Thou Endure It Well.* Salt Lake City, UT: Bookcraft, 2002.
—*Lord, Increase Our Faith.* Salt Lake City, UT: Bookcraft, 1994.
—*Men and Women of Christ.* Salt Lake City, UT: Deseret Book, 1991.
—*Notwithstanding My Weakness.* Salt Lake City, UT: Deseret Book, 1981.
—*One More Strain of Praise.* Salt Lake City, UT: Deseret Book, 2003.
—"Patience," *Ensign,* October 1980.
—*That Ye May Believe.* Salt Lake City, UT: Bookcraft, 1994.
—*The Promise of Discipleship.* Salt Lake City, UT: Deseret Book, 2001.
—"These Are Your Days," *New Era,* January 1985.
McConkie, Bruce R. *A New Witness for the Articles of Faith.* Salt Lake City, UT: Deseret Book, 1985.
—*Doctrinal New Testament Commentary.* Salt Lake City, UT: Deseret Book, 1972.
—*Doctrines of Salvation: Sermons and Writings of Joseph Fielding Smith,* Salt Lake City, UT: Bookcraft, 1954–1956.
—*Mormon Doctrine.* Salt Lake City, UT: Bookcraft: 1966.
—"Obedience, Consecration, and Sacrifice," *Ensign,* May 1975.
—"The Doctrine of the Priesthood," *Ensign,* May 1982.
—*The Mortal Messiah: From Bethlehem to Calvary.* Salt Lake City, UT: Deseret Book, 1981.

Bibliography

—"*The Probationary Test of Mortality.*" Address delivered at the University of Utah Institute, January 10, 1982.

—*The Promised Messiah: The First Coming of Christ.* Salt Lake City, UT: Deseret Book, 1981.

—"The Ten Blessings of the Priesthood," *Ensign*, November 1977.

McConkie, Joseph Fielding and Robert L. Millet. *Doctrinal Commentary on the Book of Mormon.* Salt Lake City, UT: Deseret Book, 1987–1993.

—*Joseph Smith: The Choice Seer.* Salt Lake City, UT: Bookcraft, 1996.

—*Revelations of the Restoration.* Salt Lake City, UT: Deseret Book, 2000.

McKay, David O. *Gospel Ideals: Selections from the Discourses of David O. McKay.* Salt Lake City, UT: Deseret Book, 1993.

----*Pathways to Happiness.* Salt Lake City, UT: Bookcraft, 1957.

McMullin, Keith B. "Come to Zion! Come to Zion!" Salt Lake City, UT: *Ensign*, November 2002.

Merriam Webster's New World Dictionary, Third Edition. New York, NY: Simon and Schuster, 1998

Middlemiss, Clare. *Man May Know for Himself: Teachings of President David O. McKay.* Salt Lake City, UT: Deseret Book, 1967.

Millet, Robert L. "Quest for the City of God: The Doctrine Of Zion In Modern Revelation," *1989 Sperry Symposium on the Doctrine and Covenants.* Salt Lake City, UT: Desert Book, 1989.

—*The Capstone of Our Religion: Insights into the Doctrine and Covenants.* Salt Lake City, UT: Deseret Book, 1989.

—*The Life Beyond.* Salt Lake City, UT: Deseret Book, 1986.

—*The Power of the Word: Saving Doctrines from the Book of Mormon.* Salt Lake City, UT: Deseret *Book*, 2000.

Monson, Thomas S. "In Quest of the Abundant Life." *Ensign*, March 1988.

Nelson, Russell M. "Personal Priesthood Responsibility," *Ensign*, October 2005.

—*The Power within Us.* Salt Lake City, UT: Deseret Book, 1989.

Nelson, William O. "Enoch and His Message for Latter Days," *Deseret News*, Feb. 5, 1994.

Neuenschwander, Dennis. "Ordinances and Covenants," *Ensign*, August 2001.

Nibley, Hugh. *Abraham in Egypt.* Salt Lake City, UT and Provo, UT: Deseret Book and FARMS, 2000.

—*An Approach to the Book of Mormon.* Salt Lake City, UT: Deseret Book, 1988.

—*Approaching Zion.* Salt Lake City, UT: Deseret Book, 1989.

—"Educating the Saints—A Brigham Young Mosaic." Provo, UT: *BYU Studies*, Vol. 11, Autumn 1970.

—*Nibley on the Timely and the Timeless.* Provo, UT: Religious Studies Center, Brigham Young University, 2004.

—*Teachings of the Book of Mormon.* Provo, UT: Covenant Communications, 2004.

—*Temple and Cosmos: Beyond This Ignorant Present.* Salt Lake City, UT: Deseret Book, 1992.

Nibley, Preston. *Brigham Young: The Man and His Work*, 4th ed. Salt Lake City, UT: Deseret Book, 1960.

Nielsen, Donna B. *Beloved Bridegroom.* Salt Lake City, UT: Onyx Press, 1999.

Nyman, Monte S. and Charles D. Tate, Jr., eds. *Fourth Nephi through Moroni: From Zion to Destruction.* Salt Lake City, UT: Bookcraft, 1992.

—*The Capstone of Our Religion: Insights into the Doctrine and Covenants.* Salt Lake City, UT: Bookcraft, 1989.

Oaks, Dallin H. "Good, Better, Best," *Ensign,* November 2007.

—"He Heals the Heavy Laden," *Ensign,* November 2006

—"Preparation for the Second Coming," *Ensign,* November 2004.

—"Taking Upon Us the Name of Jesus Christ," *Ensign,* May 1985.

—"The Challenge to Become," *Ensign,* November 2000.

—"Timing," *Ensign,* October 2003.

Oaks, Robert C. "The Power of Patience," *Ensign,* November 2006.

Otten, L. G. and C. M. Caldwell. *Sacred Truths of the Doctrine and Covenants.* Salt Lake City, UT: Deseret Book, 1982–1983.

Pack, Frederick J. "Was the Earth Created in Six Days of Twenty-Four Hours Each?" *Improvement Era,* October 1930.

Packer, Boyd K. "Personal Revelation: The Gift, the Test, and the Promise," *Ensign,* November 1994.

—"Restoration," *First Worldwide Leadership Training Meeting.* Salt Lake City, UT: The Church of Jesus Christ of Latter-day Saints, January 2003.

—*That All May Be Edified.* Salt Lake City, UT: Bookcraft, 1982.

—"The Candle of the Lord," *Ensign,* January 1983.

—"The One Pure Defense (An Evening with President Boyd K. Packer)," Intellectual Reserve, 2004. Address to CES Religious Educators, 6 February 2004, Salt Lake Tabernacle.

Parry, Donald W., ed. *Temples of the Ancient World: Ritual and Symbolism.* Salt Lake City, UT and Provo, UT: Deseret and FARMS, 1994.

—*Understanding the Book of Revelation.* Salt Lake City, UT: Deseret Book, 1998.

Peterson, H. Burke. "Your Special Purpose," *New Era,* October 2001.

Pratt, Orson. *Times and Seasons,* vol. 6. no. 10, 1 June 1845.

Riddle, Chauncey C. "The New and Everlasting Covenant," 1989 *Sperry Symposium on the Doctrine and Covenants.* Salt Lake City: Desert Book, 1989.

Roberts, B.H. *Comprehensive History of the Church of Jesus Christ of Latter-day Saints.* Salt Lake City, UT: Church of Jesus Christ of Latter-day Saints, 1930.

—*Seventy's Course of Theology.* Salt Lake City, UT: Deseret Book, 1931.

Romney, Marion G. "Church Welfare Services' Basic Principles," *Ensign,* May 1976.

—"Church Welfare—Temporal Service in a Spiritual Setting," *Ensign,* May 1980

—"Priesthood," *Ensign,* May 1982.

—"'In Mine Own Way,'" *Ensign,* November 1976.

—"The Celestial Nature of Self-reliance," *Ensign,* November 1982.

—"The Oath and Covenant Which Belongeth to the Priesthood," *Ensign,* November 1980.

—"The Purpose of Church Welfare Services," *Ensign,* May 1977.

—"The Royal Law of Love," *Ensign*, May 1978.
—"Unity," *Ensign*, May 1983.
—"Welfare Services: The Savior's Program," *Ensign*, October 1980.
Salt Lake School of the Prophets Minutes. Salt Lake City, UT: The Church of Jesus Christ of Latter-day Saints, 1899.
"Sermon Given to Different People," *LDS Church News*, Feb. 18, 1995.
Skidmore, Rex A. "What Part Should a Teenager Play in a Family?" *Improvement Era*, 1952.
Skinner, Andrew C. *Temple Worship: 20 Truths That Will Bless Your Life*. Salt Lake City, UT: Deseret Book, 2008.
—*The Old Testament and the Latter-Day Saints*. Salt Lake City, UT: Deseret Book, 2005.
Smith, Hyrum M. and Janne M. Sjodahl. *Doctrine and Covenants Commentary*. Salt Lake City, UT: Deseret Book, 1960.
Smith, Joseph. *Evening and Morning Star*, July, 1833.
—*History of The Church of Jesus Christ of Latter-day Saints*. Salt Lake City, UT: Deseret Book, 1980.
—*Lectures on Faith*. Salt Lake City, UT: Deseret Book, 1993.
Smith, Joseph F. *Gospel Doctrine: Selections from the Sermons and Writings of Joseph F. Smith*. Deseret News Press, 1919.
—*Teachings of Presidents of the Church*. Salt Lake City, UT: The Church of Jesus Christ of Latter-day Saints, 1998.
Smith, Joseph Fielding. *Church History and Modern Revelation*. Salt Lake City, UT: The Church of Jesus Christ of Latter-day Saints, 1946.
—"Our responsibility as Priesthood Holders," *Ensign*, June 1971.
—*Teachings of the Prophet Joseph Smith*. Salt Lake City, UT: Deseret Book, 1938.
—"The Duties of the Priesthood in Temple Work," *The Utah Genealogical and Historical Magazine*, vol. 30, no. 1, January 1939.
—*The Restoration of All Things*. Salt Lake City, UT: Deseret News Press, 1945.
Snow, Lorenzo. *The Teachings of Lorenzo Snow*, Salt Lake City, UT: Bookcraft, 1984.
Sorensen, A. D. "No Respecter of Persons: Equality in the Kingdom." ed. Mary E. Stoval, .*As Women of Faith: Talks Selected from the BYU Women's Conferences*. Salt Lake City, UT: Deseret Book, 1989, 55.
Stevenson, Edward. "Life and History of Elder Edward Stevenson." Provo, UT: Special Collections, Harold B. Lee Library, Brigham Young University, n.d.
Stuy, Brian H., comp., *Collected Discourses*. Burbank, CA: B.H.S. Publishing, 1988.
Summerhays, James T. "The Stripling Elect." *MeridianMagazine.com*, February 20, 2009.
Talmage, James E. *Articles of Faith*. Salt Lake City, UT: Deseret Book, 1984.
—*Jesus the Christ*. Salt Lake City: Deseret News Press, 1915.
—"The Eternity of Sex," *Young Woman's Journal*, October 1914.
—*The House of the Lord*. Salt Lake City, UT: Bookcraft, 1962.
Tanakh: A New Translation of the Holy Scriptures According to the Traditional Hebrew Text. Philadelphia, PA: Jewish Publication Society of America, November 1985.
Tanner, N. Eldon. "Constancy Amid Change," Ensign, November 1979.

Tanner, Susan W. "All Things Shall Work Together for Your Good," *Ensign,* May 2004.
—"My Soul Delighteth in the Things of the Lord," *Ensign,* 2008.
Taylor, John. *Teachings of the Latter-day Prophets.* Salt Lake City, UT: Bookcraft, 1998.
Times and Seasons, vol. 6. no. 10, 1 June 1845.
Thomas, M. Catherine. "Alma the Younger, Part 1," Provo, UT: Neal A. Maxwell Institute for Religious Scholarship, 1996.
—"Alma the Younger, Part 2," Provo, UT: Neal A. Maxwell Institute for Religious Scholarship, 1996.
—"Benjamin and the Mysteries of God," *King Benjamin's Speech.* Provo, UT: Foundation for Ancient Research and Mormon Studies, 1998.
Turner, Rodney. *Woman and the Priesthood.* Salt Lake City, UT: Deseret Book, 1972.
Tvedtnes, John A. *The Church of the Old Testament.* Salt Lake City, UT: Deseret Book, 1967.
—"They Have Their Reward." *MeridianMagazine.com,* February 21, 2007.
Van Orden, Bruce A. and Brent L. Top. *Doctrines of the Book of Mormon: The 1991 Sperry Symposium,* Provo, UT: Maxwell Institute, 1993.
Watt, George D., ed. *Journal of Discourses.* Liverpool, England: F.D. Richards, et al., 1854–1886.
Whitney, Newell K. in *Messenger and Advocate,* 3 September 1837.
Whitney, Orson F. *Gospel Themes.* Salt Lake City, UT: n.p., 1914.
—*Life of Heber C. Kimball.* Salt Lake City, UT: Bookcraft, 1975.
—*Saturday Night Thoughts.* Salt Lake City, UT: Deseret News, 1927.
Wickman, Lance B. "Today," *Ensign,* May 2008.
Widtsoe, John A. *An Understandable Religion.* Salt Lake City, UT: The Church of Jesus Christ of Latter-day Saints, 1944.
—*Priesthood and Church Government.* Salt Lake City, UT: Deseret Book, 1939.
—*Utah Genealogical and Historical Magazine.* Salt Lake City, UT: October 1934.
Williams, Clyde J. *The Teachings of Lorenzo Snow, Fifth President of the Church of Jesus Christ of Latter-day Saints.* Salt Lake City, UT: Bookcraft, 1984.
Wilson, Marvin. *Our Father Abraham,* Grand Rapids, MI: Eerdmans Publishing Co., 1989.
Winder, Barbara W. "Finding Joy in Life," *Ensign,* November 1987.
Wirthlin, Joseph B. "The Great Commandment," *Ensign,* November 2007.
—"The Law of the Fast," *Ensign,* May 2001.
Woodruff, Wilford. *The Discourses of Wilford Woodruff.* Salt Lake City, UT: Bookcraft, 1946.
Yarn, David H. *The Gospel: God, Man, and Truth.* Salt Lake City, UT: Deseret Book, 1965.
Yorgason, Blaine M. *I Need Thee Every Hour.* Salt Lake City, UT: Deseret Book, 2003.
—*Spiritual Progression in the Last Days.* Salt Lake City, UT: Deseret Book, 1994.
Young, Brigham in *Deseret News,* 10 October 1866.
—*Discourses of Brigham Young.* Salt Lake City, UT: Deseret Book, 1926.
—*Journal History.* 28 September 1846.
—*Millennial Star, Vol. 16.* Salt Lake City, UT: The Church of Jesus Christ of Latter-day Saints, 1840–1970.

Index and Concordance

This is a master index of the book series. The page number is specific to the book in which it is located. For example: 101:3 means page 101 in book 3. Marker "P" refers to Portrait of a Zion Person.

Aaronic Priesthood. *See* **Oath and Covenant of the Priesthood;** *See* **Patriarchal Order of the Priesthood;** *See* **Priesthood**
    40:2, 41:2, 12:3, 22:3, 23:3, 36:3, 39:3, 42:3, 59:3, 60:3, 76:3, 92:3, 93:3, 103:3, 104:3, 202:3, 204:3, 50:4, 131:5

abundance
    5:6, 8:6, 10:6, 13:6, 17:6, 18:6, 31:6, 41:6, 44:6, 46:6, 52:6, 70:6, 82:6, 87:6, 96:6, 101:6, 103:6, 106:6, 107:6, 110:6, 111:6, 112:6, 114:6, 115:6

Adam
    empowered to become a savior to his family
        11:1

adultery. *See also* **immoral**
    Babylon distinguished by
        50:2

adversary. *See also* **devil;** *See also* **hell;** *See also* **Lucifer;** *See also* **Satan**
    attacks Saints more viciously than others
        44:1

adversity
    33:2, 51:2, 54:2, 56:2, 58:2, 61:2, 34:3, 66:3, 117:3, 132:3, 186:3, 178:4, 10:5, 27:5, 30:5, 76:5, 50:6, 101:6 *See also* opposition; *See also* trial(s)

affluence. *See also* **mammon;** *See also* **riches;** *See also* **wealth**
    85:1, 139:4, 103:5, 64:6, 71:6

agency
    a discussion of
        62–68:4

Amulek
    52:1, 80:1, 51:2, 52:2, 55:3, 42:4, 59:4, 133:4, 180:4, 36:5, 71:5, 56:6, 104:6

angels
    involved in crucible experiences
        26:5

anger. *See also* **contention**
    19:1, 57:1, 64:1, 75:1, 86:1, 87:1, 93:1, 96:1, 97:1, 98:1, 55:2, 23:3, 152:3, 169:3, 176:3, 5:4, 29:4, 34:4, 101:4, 111:4, 116:4, 121:4, 136:4, 165:4, 179:4, 180:4, 4:5, 15:5, 22:5, 41:5, 46:5, 79:5, 104:5, 107:5, 124:5, 17:6, 28:6, 34:6, 39:6, 60:6, 94:6, 116:6

anti-Christ
    17:P, 21:1, 49:1, 50:1, 51:1, 61:1, 79:1, 84:1, 85:1, 101:1, 54:2, 67:3, 87:4, 127:4, 175:4, 176:4, 33:5, 48:5, 7:6, 47:6, 88:6

apostasy
    27:1, 33:1, 34:1, 60:1, 68:1, 84:4, 108:5

apostle
    59:1, 17:2

Index & Concordance

Atonement
6:P, 14:P, 15:P, 24:P, 42:P, 11:1, 12:1, 22:1, 23:1, 42:1, 45:1, 47:1, 66:1, 70:1, 1:2, 3:2, 6:2, 7:2, 9:2, 10:2, 16:2, 17:2, 18:2, 19:2, 20:2, 23:2, 24:2, 25:2, 26:2, 27:2, 28:2, 29:2, 30:2, 31:2, 32:2, 34:2, 35:2, 36:2, 37:2, 38:2, 39:2, 45:2, 55:2, 57:2, 66:2, 67:2, 72:2, 93:2, 98:2, 1:3, 10:3, 17:3, 20:3, 21:3, 35:3, 63:3, 70:3, 73:3, 76:3, 158:3, 180:3, 196:3, 211:3, 214:3, 1:4, 16:4, 18:4, 19:4, 20:4, 31:4, 41:4, 42:4, 56:4, 57:4, 59:4, 64:4, 99:4, 122:4, 162:4, 185:4, 1:5, 4:5, 29:5, 64:5, 84:5, 87:5, 91:5, 106:5, 107:5, 111:5, 113:5, 117:5, 129:5, 133:5, 137:5, 15:6, 42:6, 67:6, 75:6

Babel
> a counterfeit gate of God
> > 54:1
>
> Nimrod established kingdom in
> > 53:1

Babylon. *See also* **world**
> a discussion of
> > 49–105:1
>
> state of mind defined by excess, self-indulgence
> > 54:1

baptism
2:P, 18:P, 21:P, 25:P, 11:1, 19:1, 23:1, 9:2, 18:2, 19:2, 21:2, 28:2, 31:2, 33:2, 34:2, 35:2, 36:2, 37:2, 38:2, 40:2, 41:2, 44:2, 45:2, 49:2, 53:2, 60:2, 63:2, 64:2, 67:2, 68:2, 70:2, 73:2, 75:2, 81:2, 82:2, 91:2, 93:2, 98:2, 1:3, 2:3, 4:3, 5:3, 9:3, 10:3, 11:3, 17:3, 21:3, 23:3, 27:3, 39:3, 42:3, 66:3, 70:3, 71:3, 76:3, 80:3, 93:3, 99:3, 117:3, 143:3, 144:3, 153:3, 179:3, 187:3, 193:3, 200:3, 210:3, 214:3, 1:4, 14:4, 26:4, 39:4, 51:4, 52:4, 88:4, 142:4, 144:4, 145:4, 1:5, 17:5, 18:5, 60:5, 61:5, 62:5, 63:5, 82:5, 83:5, 106:5, 117:5, 133:5, 134:5, 135:5, 68:6, 75:6, 76:6, 106:6

Beatitudes. *See also* **Sermon on the Mount**
16:P, 18:P, 28:P, 28:1, 49:3, 41:5, 82:5

believe. *See* **faith**
> in order to see
> > 68:5

Beloved Son. *See also* **Christ**; *See also* **Exemplar**; *See also* **Jehovah**; *See also* **Lamb**; *See also* **Savior**
47:1, 65:3, 111:3, 55:5, 56:5, 110:5, 115:5

Bible
39:1, 63:1, 83:1, 54:2, 7:3, 138:3, 153:3, 203:3, 8:5

blasphemy
59:1, 82:3

bloodline
> men ordained to priesthood regardless of
> > 17:1

Book of Mormon
> 12:P, 19:P, 21:P, 30:P, 39:P, 42:P, 1:1, 2:1, 5:1, 12:1, 17:1, 31:1, 34:1, 37:1, 61:1, 64:1, 67:1, 70:1, 78:1, 103:1, 18:2, 51:2, 7:3, 17:3, 19:3, 45:3, 46:3, 69:3, 70:3, 92:3, 120:3, 123:3, 132:3, 141:3, 146:3, 153:3, 163:3, 171:3, 180:3, 5:4, 26:4, 40:4, 69:4, 85:4, 97:4, 99:4, 104:4, 108:4, 124:4, 135:4, 138:4, 139:4, 157:4, 161:4, 4:5, 8:5, 11:5, 23:5, 34:5, 59:5, 78:5, 96:5, 103:5, 109:5, 118:5, 127:5, 129:5, 11:6, 15:6, 20:6, 25:6, 44:6, 59:6, 61:6, 63:6, 113:6

Bridegroom. *See also* Christ, Jesus
> 75:1, 85:1, 58:2, 71:2, 72:2, 73:2, 74:2, 75:2, 76:2, 77:2, 78:2, 79:2, 80:2, 81:2, 82:2, 83:2, 84:2, 85:2, 86:2, 87:2, 88:2, 89:2, 90:2, 91:2, 92:2, 93:2, 94:2, 95:2, 96:2, 97:2, 98:2, 111:3, 161:3, 173:3, 183:3, 98:4, 11:6

Brigham Young
> 14:P, 26:P, 39:P, 41:P, 3:1, 5:1, 6:1, 12:1, 39:1, 40:1, 44:1, 46:1, 90:1, 103:1, 1:2, 61:2, 1:3, 3:3, 19:3, 56:3, 96:3, 101:3, 102:3, 127:3, 128:3, 142:3, 164:3, 192:3, 193:3, 201:3, 214:3, 1:4, 10:4, 30:4, 47:4, 62:4, 75:4, 85:4, 87:4, 89:4, 97:4, 105:4, 106:4, 109:4, 113:4, 125:4, 131:4, 132:4, 133:4, 135:4, 137:4, 140:4, 141:4, 149:4, 150:4, 152:4, 1:5, 4:5, 11:5, 28:5, 41:5, 56:5, 73:5, 81:5, 84:5, 90:5, 91:5, 96:5, 97:5, 99:5, 101:5, 109:5, 127:5, 134:5, 136:5, 137:5, 11:6, 20:6, 21:6, 27:6, 30:6, 31:6, 45:6, 55:6, 56:6, 57:6, 58:6, 59:6, 61:6, 64:6, 65:6, 71:6, 105:6

brother of Jared
> 13:1, 74:1, 58:2, 184:3, 196:3, 209:3, 210:3, 8:5, 21:5, 29:5, 32:5, 34:5, 41:5, 43:5, 53:5, 58:5, 66:5, 68:5, 69:5, 70:5, 73:5, 86:5, 112:5, 119:5

Bruce R. McConkie
> 34:P, 36:P, 37:P, 11:1, 45:1, 85:2, 93:2, 2:3, 9:3, 11:3, 14:3, 21:3, 25:3, 33:3, 79:3, 214:3, 2:4, 8:4, 62:4, 68:4, 82:4, 135:4, 2:5, 7:5, 60:5, 64:5, 129:5, 58:6

business. *See* mammon

Cain
> 13:1, 51:1, 52:1, 53:1, 54:1, 61:1, 69:1, 72:1, 74:1, 77:1, 79:1, 90:1, 101:1, 109:3, 82:4, 127:4, 150:4, 175:4, 176:4, 47:6, 88:6

calling and election made sure
>> chronology of
>>> 83:3

carnal
> 20:P, 25:P, 41:P, 19:1, 23:1, 59:1, 62:1, 70:1, 89:1, 94:1, 101:1, 102:1, 8:2, 23:2, 25:2, 29:2, 33:2, 62:2, 23:3, 109:3, 172:3, 178:3, 64:4, 65:4, 100:4, 109:4, 149:4, 14:5, 44:5, 67:5, 93:5, 16:6, 26:6, 76:6

celestial kingdom
> 14:P, 16:P, 18:P, 22:P, 28:P, 34:P, 48:1, 14:2, 15:2, 16:2, 18:2, 21:2, 27:2, 37:2, 74:2, 2:3, 22:3, 23:3, 28:3, 34:3, 69:3, 71:3, 79:3, 103:3, 115:3, 121:3, 124:3, 125:3, 153:3, 168:3, 182:3, 186:3, 199:3, 2:4, 3:4, 4:4, 6:4, 8:4, 10:4, 15:4, 26:4, 29:4, 30:4, 38:4, 51:4, 52:4, 54:4, 63:4, 68:4, 73:4, 77:4, 79:4, 89:4, 90:4, 91:4, 95:4, 126:4, 132:4, 141:4, 144:4, 148:4, 150:4, 152:4, 185:4, 2:5, 11:5, 31:5, 50:5, 78:5, 120:5, 132:5, 134:5, 135:5, 3:6, 6:6, 9:6, 13:6, 31:6, 46:6, 56:6, 66:6, 68:6, 72:6, 94:6, 105:6, 110:6

charity
> a discussion of
>> 165–184:4
>
> characteristics of
>> 147–173:3

chaste
> 5:2, 22:2, 66:2, 24:5, 57:5

Christ, Jesus. *See also* **Beloved Son**; *See also* **Exemplar**; *See also* **Jehovah**; *See also* **Lamb**; *See also* **Savior**
> a discussion of
>> as Bridegroom
>>> 72–98:2
>>
>> coming into his presence
>>> 77:2
>>
>> taking name of, upon us
>>> 59:2
>
> frees us from the powers of Babylon
>> 26:1

city of Enoch
> 14:1, 16:1, 36:1, 5:3, 19:3, 23:5, 34:5, 72:5, 2:6

comforter. *See also* **Holy Ghost**
> 37:2, 86:2, 71:3

commerce. *See also* **mammon**
> 76:1, 79:1

compete, competition
> 79:1, 88:1, 119:3, 132:3

consecrate, consecration
> a discussion of
>> blessings of living
>>> 33–50:4
>>
>> characteristics of the law of
>>> 3–31:4
>>
>> guiding principles of
>>> 62–91:4
>
> living law of, brings blessings of abundance
>> 18:1
>
> to set apart
>> 160:4

contention. *See also* **anger**
> 6:P, 12:P, 43:P, 19:1, 21:1, 24:1, 29:1, 64:1, 67:1, 79:1, 85:1, 88:1, 102:1, 8:3, 119:3, 128:3, 42:4, 48:4, 179:4, 180:4, 4:5, 43:5, 102:5, 103:5, 104:5, 107:5, 108:5, 2:6, 117:6

cooperate
    25:P, 6:2, 9:2, 100:5
corn
    kernel of, represents potential of grace freely given
        55:3
coronation
    1:2, 9:2, 98:2, 29:3, 30:3, 36:3, 184:3, 194:3, 195:3, 65:5, 73:5, 135:5
counterfeit
    Satan always has, to God's works
        61:1
covet
    36:P, 24:1, 70:1, 69:4, 86:4, 100:4, 102:4, 148:4, 16:6, 17:6, 18:6, 115:6
Creator. See **Christ, Jesus**
crown. See **coronation**
crucibles
    angels involved in
        26:5
    many, last fourteen years
        25:5
deceive. See **deception**
deception
    victims of, will not be condemned
        22:1
Deity. See **God**
deliverance
    20:P, 18:1, 25:1, 72:1, 8:2, 22:2, 35:2, 51:2, 52:2, 26:3, 121:3, 128:3, 140:3, 148:3, 44:4, 84:4, 125:4, 131:4, 161:4, 162:4, 163:4, 174:4, 178:4, 180:4, 185:4, 3:5, 16:5, 17:5, 19:5, 23:5, 26:5, 27:5, 29:5, 36:5, 38:5, 39:5, 40:5, 45:5, 48:5, 49:5, 50:5, 51:5, 52:5, 55:5, 57:5, 68:5, 69:5, 70:5, 71:5, 72:5, 73:5, 75:5, 76:5, 78:5, 45:6, 52:6, 101:6
descend
    we must, below all things to ascend above all
        39:1
devil. See also **adversary**; See also **hell**; See also **Lucifer**; See also **Satan**
    6:P, 35:P, 41:P, 21:1, 24:1, 44:1, 51:1, 52:1, 60:1, 61:1, 62:1, 63:1, 64:1, 68:1, 70:1, 72:1, 73:1, 84:1, 86:1, 90:1, 92:1, 100:1, 101:1, 102:1, 28:2, 32:2, 49:2, 89:2, 98:2, 97:3, 109:3, 131:3, 160:3, 163:3, 172:3, 188:3, 189:3, 19:4, 45:4, 63:4, 64:4, 65:4, 67:4, 70:4, 109:4, 113:4, 120:4, 138:4, 141:4, 149:4, 151:4, 152:4, 14:5, 18:5, 47:5, 55:5, 101:5, 104:5, 107:5, 120:5, 26:6, 27:6, 30:6, 38:6, 63:6, 65:6, 71:6, 117:6
disputations
    6:P, 17:P, 26:P, 30:1, 49:1, 57:1, 19:3, 42:4, 119:4, 107:5, 108:5, 109:5, 122:5, 2:6, 37:6, 117:6

Index & Concordance

elect
    57:1, 63:1, 85:1, 101:1, 103:1, 43:2, 48:2, 92:2, 40:3, 63:3, 79:3, 80:3, 81:3, 82:3, 84:3, 85:3, 87:3, 105:3, 114:3, 140:3, 154:3, 203:3, 73:5, 74:5, 90:5, 96:5, 7:6

Elijah
    23:P, 35:P, 31:1, 81:2, 12:3, 13:3, 14:3, 15:3, 16:3, 17:3, 65:3, 116:3, 121:3, 66:4, 130:4, 8:5, 51:5, 70:5, 92:5, 52:6

Eliza R. Snow
    34:1

endow, endowment
    Abraham administered, regardless of bloodline
        17:1

Enoch
    3:P, 12:P, 15:P, 33:P, 37:P, 39:P, 3:1, 4:1, 6:1, 7:1, 13:1, 14:1, 15:1, 16:1, 18:1, 32:1, 33:1, 36:1, 37:1, 55:1, 58:1, 74:1, 87:1, 88:1, 103:1, 11:2, 12:2, 5:3, 7:3, 9:3, 18:3, 19:3, 20:3, 24:3, 25:3, 27:3, 30:3, 46:3, 57:3, 72:3, 73:3, 89:3, 93:3, 116:3, 184:3, 198:3, 204:3, 207:3, 208:3, 209:3, 10:4, 11:4, 82:4, 86:4, 157:4, 23:5, 34:5, 37:5, 69:5, 72:5, 86:5, 89:5, 90:5, 94:5, 96:5, 100:5, 101:5, 112:5, 124:5, 125:5, 127:5, 132:5, 1:6, 2:6

equal
    6:P, 7:P, 12:P, 33:P, 27:1, 41:1, 57:1, 65:1, 87:1, 13:2, 64:2, 4:3, 18:3, 40:3, 41:3, 50:3, 60:3, 90:3, 105:3, 106:3, 119:3, 132:3, 200:3, 9:4, 24:4, 26:4, 27:4, 30:4, 36:4, 37:4, 38:4, 39:4, 49:4, 58:4, 59:4, 61:4, 73:4, 74:4, 77:4, 90:4, 96:4, 125:4, 156:4, 183:4, 185:4, 4:5, 122:5, 123:5, 3:6, 10:6, 45:6, 53:6, 77:6, 107:6, 116:6

exalt
    25:P, 1:2, 9:2, 32:2, 33:2, 45:2, 54:2, 57:2, 61:2, 28:3, 59:3, 132:3, 134:3, 142:3, 146:3, 4:4, 37:4, 52:4, 56:4, 109:4, 184:4, 93:5, 26:6, 76:6, 78:6, 108:6, 116:6

Exemplar. *See also* **Christ, Jesus**; *See also* **Jehovah**; *See also* **Lamb**; *See also* **Savior**
    39:1, 65:3

Ezra Taft Benson
    34:P, 8:1, 24:1, 41:1, 61:1, 67:1, 26:3, 109:3, 116:3, 205:3, 6:4, 15:4, 25:4, 26:4, 27:4, 28:4, 48:4, 59:4, 1:6, 80:6, 105:6

face-to-face
    coming, with God is ultimate blessing and right of Zion people
        97:3

family, families
    3:P, 4:P, 23:P, 27:P, 29:P, 31:P, 32:P, 33:P, 34:P, 36:P, 37:P, 38:P, 42:P, 43:P, 6:1, 11:1, 12:1, 13:1, 14:1, 17:1, 18:1, 24:1, 26:1, 40:1, 42:1, 43:1, 45:1, 47:1, 54:1, 89:1, 93:1, 5:2, 23:2, 29:2, 32:2, 36:2, 37:2, 41:2, 50:2, 51:2, 52:2, 53:2, 62:2, 64:2, 68:2, 80:2, 83:2, 92:2, 5:3, 8:3, 12:3, 13:3, 14:3, 15:3, 16:3, 17:3, 20:3, 25:3, 26:3, 27:3, 28:3, 31:3, 32:3, 34:3, 65:3, 69:3, 70:3, 76:3, 78:3, 92:3, 100:3, 111:3, 113:3, 120:3, 136:3, 139:3, 146:3, 170:3, 178:3, 185:3, 186:3, 199:3, 200:3, 201:3, 204:3, 206:3, 207:3, 212:3, 4:4, 6:4, 8:4, 9:4, 23:4, 26:4, 27:4, 29:4, 30:4, 39:4, 41:4, 69:4, 72:4, 73:4,

74:4, 79:4, 82:4, 84:4, 86:4, 87:4, 133:4, 134:4, 141:4, 151:4, 157:4, 170:4, 171:4, 179:4, 180:4, 4:5, 21:5, 24:5, 42:5, 50:5, 51:5, 52:5, 62:5, 66:5, 71:5, 94:5, 95:5, 104:5, 107:5, 127:5, 133:5, 134:5, 5:6, 57:6, 65:6, 78:6, 87:6, 98:6, 102:6, 103:6, 104:6, 111:6, 112:6, 113:6, 114:6, 115:6

fathers
6:P, 18:1, 28:1, 35:1, 45:1, 63:1, 81:1, 91:1, 98:1, 32:2, 75:2, 13:3, 15:3, 17:3, 23:3, 27:3, 65:3, 77:3, 91:3, 104:3, 160:3, 161:3, 207:3, 118:4, 124:4, 128:4, 137:4, 141:4, 152:4, 67:5, 109:5, 124:5, 128:5, 136:5, 4:6, 37:6, 43:6, 48:6, 60:6, 66:6

fear
11:P, 26:P, 29:P, 42:P, 43:P, 23:1, 35:1, 37:1, 40:1, 53:1, 56:1, 64:1, 84:1, 85:1, 93:1, 94:1, 97:1, 59:2, 86:2, 39:3, 128:3, 130:3, 142:3, 149:3, 158:3, 169:3, 186:3, 196:3, 4:4, 22:4, 116:4, 141:4, 171:4, 172:4, 177:4, 27:5, 37:5, 57:5, 101:5, 133:5, 1:6, 35:6, 66:6, 90:6, 97:6, 98:6, 112:6

flatter
73:1, 96:1

forgive
10:P, 39:2, 40:2, 116:4, 178:4, 183:4, 35:6, 101:6

fornication
56:1, 57:1, 58:1, 59:1, 76:1, 80:1, 93:1, 50:2, 22:5

fourteen years
> many crucibles last
>> 25:5

fruit
> ripe, falls from tree of life to rot on ground
>> 96:1

fundamentalism
> definition of
>> 83:1

Gadianton robbers. *See also* **secret combinations**
> 97:1

Garden of Eden
> 13:1, 77:1, 108:4, 8:5, 28:5, 36:5, 72:5, 25:6

gathering
> always associated with Zion
>> 20:1

generosity. *See* **selflessness**

give yourself rich. *See* **abundance**
> 8:P, 176:4, 89:6

God-like, godliness
> become, by learning how to lift others
>> 5:1

Index & Concordance

gold
    28:P, 38:P, 42:P, 27:1, 50:1, 52:1, 58:1, 59:1, 62:1, 76:1, 96:1, 22:2, 80:2, 94:2, 129:3, 151:3, 9:4, 40:4, 44:4, 82:4, 101:4, 103:4, 106:4, 109:4, 116:4, 118:4, 124:4, 132:4, 139:4, 140:4, 145:4, 146:4, 3:5, 21:5, 23:5, 24:5, 25:5, 26:5, 17:6, 19:6, 22:6, 27:6, 35:6, 36:6, 44:6, 55:6, 64:6, 65:6, 68:6, 69:6, 70:6

good
    definition of
        9:1

goods. *See* mammon

Gordon B. Hinckley
    6:P, 7:1, 28:2, 55:3, 172:3, 211:3, 37:4, 40:4, 41:4, 56:4, 59:4, 60:4, 164:4, 170:4, 87:5, 78:6, 83:6, 93:6

grace. *See also* mercy
    15:P, 19:P, 22:P, 4:1, 6:1, 10:1, 11:1, 28:1, 42:1, 4:2, 17:2, 18:2, 19:2, 20:2, 22:2, 23:2, 26:2, 29:2, 36:2, 38:2, 43:2, 45:2, 78:2, 16:3, 21:3, 24:3, 52:3, 53:3, 54:3, 55:3, 60:3, 64:3, 86:3, 104:3, 153:3, 198:3, 200:3, 57:4, 66:4, 79:4, 89:4, 92:4, 139:4, 146:4, 174:4, 175:4, 177:4, 181:4, 184:4, 7:5, 20:5, 31:5, 32:5, 45:5, 90:5, 124:5, 64:6, 70:6, 75:6, 80:6, 81:6, 82:6, 83:6, 89:6, 90:6, 100:6, 101:6

Harold B. Lee
    16:P, 28:P, 28:1, 82:1, 49:3, 130:3, 131:3, 204:3, 82:5, 147:5

heal
    21:P, 1:1, 2:1, 46:1, 135:3, 142:3, 152:3, 165:3, 171:3, 73:4, 77:4, 142:4, 144:4, 159:4, 160:4, 161:4, 184:4, 15:5, 113:5, 68:6, 86:6

healing
    we prepare for Zion by experiencing
        160:4

health
    23:P, 9:1, 76:1, 90:1, 100:1, 24:2, 29:2, 123:3, 18:4, 161:4, 180:4, 185:4, 15:5, 24:5, 25:5, 37:5, 57:5, 71:5, 72:5, 1:6, 86:6, 103:6, 109:6

heart
    a discussion of
        pure in
            77–108:5
    is altar of soul
        49:5
    must be changed to attain Zion
        12:1

Heber C. Kimball
    114:1, 83:3, 100:3, 101:3, 148:5

heir
    11:1, 53:1, 101:1, 29:3, 76:3, 195:3, 45:5

hell. *See also* **adversary;** *See also* **devil;** *See also* **Lucifer;** *See also* **Satan**
>18:P, 41:P, 47:1, 63:1, 68:1, 70:1, 72:1, 73:1, 74:1, 101:1, 102:1, 26:2, 97:3, 109:3, 128:3, 131:3, 154:3, 160:3, 163:3, 188:3, 75:4, 109:4, 112:4, 113:4, 120:4, 126:4, 141:4, 149:4, 13:5, 14:5, 47:5, 56:5, 97:5, 5:6, 26:6, 29:6, 30:6, 39:6, 46:6, 65:6

Holy Ghost. *See also* **comforter**
> presence of, signifies we are retaining remission of sins
>> 38:2

homosexuality
> 56:1

Hugh Nibley
> 5:P, 26:P, 33:P, 5:1, 7:1, 8:1, 33:1, 34:1, 50:1, 51:1, 56:1, 57:1, 70:1, 71:1, 75:1, 77:1, 79:1, 80:1, 89:1, 92:1, 93:1, 47:3, 109:3, 110:3, 137:3, 6:4, 7:4, 16:4, 28:4, 50:4, 56:4, 85:4, 87:4, 93:4, 94:4, 98:4, 99:4, 105:4, 108:4, 110:4, 113:4, 127:4, 132:4, 136:4, 138:4, 150:4, 21:5, 22:5, 96:5, 7:6, 8:6, 12:6, 15:6, 21:6, 25:6, 27:6, 30:6, 47:6, 56:6, 59:6, 61:6, 105:6, 116:6

hundredfold
> 8:P, 25:2, 27:2, 29:2, 123:3, 126:3, 127:3, 141:3, 151:3, 36:4, 58:4, 67:4, 92:4, 145:4, 153:4, 170:4, 177:4, 184:4, 70:5, 118:5, 3:6, 6:6, 69:6, 70:6, 72:6, 87:6, 89:6, 106:6, 107:6, 108:6, 109:6, 110:6

husband. *See also* **marriage**
> 24:2, 66:2, 75:2, 76:2, 77:2, 78:2, 79:2, 80:2, 81:2, 83:2, 84:2, 85:2, 89:2, 90:2, 94:2, 97:2, 13:3, 15:3, 17:3, 23:3, 59:3, 64:3, 85:3, 110:3, 136:3, 179:3, 183:3, 198:3, 211:3, 41:4, 43:4, 98:4, 155:4, 156:4, 157:4, 42:5, 117:5, 11:6

hypocrisy
> 80:1, 41:2, 44:3, 47:3, 108:3, 110:3, 119:3, 159:3, 160:3, 165:3, 167:3, 140:4, 64:6

idleness
> 38:P, 27:1, 56:1, 119:3, 129:3, 20:4, 39:4, 83:4, 84:4, 85:4, 86:4, 101:4, 121:4, 157:4, 18:6, 41:6, 50:6

idolatrous
> 54:1, 88:1, 54:2, 171:3, 109:4, 117:4, 27:6, 35:6

immoral. *See also* **adultery**
> 58:1, 69:1, 76:1, 87:1, 171:3, 172:3, 176:4, 88:6

inequality
> 7:P, 86:1, 114:3, 124:3, 132:3, 139:3, 19:4, 29:4, 36:4, 39:4, 73:4, 85:4, 119:4, 124:4, 125:4, 150:4, 103:5, 38:6, 44:6, 45:6, 78:6

inherit, inheritance
> a discussion of the chosen few
>> 63–105:3

Israel
> 26:P, 18:1, 29:1, 32:1, 36:1, 42:1, 43:1, 45:1, 46:1, 65:1, 100:1, 14:2, 72:2, 81:2, 90:2, 91:2, 94:2, 14:3, 23:3, 31:3, 70:3, 76:3, 77:3, 111:3, 176:3, 180:3, 196:3, 18:4, 73:4, 100:4, 101:4, 104:4, 106:4, 126:4, 130:4, 131:4, 135:4, 150:4, 160:4, 35:5, 36:5, 41:5, 79:5, 110:5, 111:5, 112:5, 113:5, 114:5, 132:5, 4:6, 16:6, 17:6, 20:6, 21:6, 22:6, 46:6, 52:6, 58:6

James E. Faust
    8:P, 83:1, 93:3, 117:3, 43:4, 156:4, 162:4, 45:5, 91:5, 142:5

Jehovah. *See also* **Christ, Jesus;** *See also* **Exemplar;** *See also* **Lamb;** *See also* **Savior**
    18:1, 30:3, 66:4, 98:4, 100:4, 88:5, 98:5, 12:6, 16:6

Jerusalem. *See also* **Salem**
    14:P, 2:1, 9:1, 15:1, 16:1, 33:1, 36:1, 37:1, 47:1, 53:1, 55:1, 61:1, 75:1, 78:1, 104:1, 1:2, 3:2, 51:2, 97:2, 1:3, 9:3, 18:3, 49:3, 100:3, 202:3, 1:4, 41:4, 1:5, 8:5, 20:5, 23:5, 63:5, 73:5, 87:5, 96:5, 97:5, 98:5, 113:5, 117:5, 118:5, 127:5, 128:5, 131:5, 134:5, 1:6

John A. Widtsoe
    8:1, 45:1, 61:1, 72:2, 164:4, 67:5, 93:6

Joseph Fielding Smith
    14:1, 81:1, 15:3, 21:3, 41:3, 56:3, 78:3, 102:3, 103:3, 190:3, 194:3, 208:3, 3:6

Joseph Smith
    4:P, 12:P, 18:P, 33:P, 39:P, 40:P, 41:P, 3:1, 5:1, 15:1, 26:1, 31:1, 32:1, 41:1, 44:1, 46:1, 48:1, 65:1, 67:1, 72:1, 90:1, 94:1, 103:1, 1:2, 3:2, 4:2, 6:2, 10:2, 15:2, 22:2, 23:2, 25:2, 26:2, 27:2, 28:2, 31:2, 42:2, 44:2, 45:2, 50:2, 58:2, 61:2, 62:2, 63:2, 87:2, 88:2, 90:2, 1:3, 5:3, 6:3, 7:3, 12:3, 13:3, 14:3, 15:3, 16:3, 17:3, 18:3, 20:3, 22:3, 25:3, 30:3, 31:3, 36:3, 43:3, 44:3, 57:3, 68:3, 69:3, 77:3, 81:3, 82:3, 83:3, 85:3, 86:3, 87:3, 88:3, 91:3, 93:3, 97:3, 98:3, 99:3, 100:3, 101:3, 104:3, 116:3, 120:3, 122:3, 125:3, 126:3, 140:3, 141:3, 160:3, 166:3, 177:3, 181:3, 182:3, 184:3, 188:3, 190:3, 191:3, 192:3, 193:3, 195:3, 196:3, 198:3, 200:3, 202:3, 203:3, 207:3, 208:3, 1:4, 4:4, 7:4, 10:4, 11:4, 12:4, 13:4, 28:4, 29:4, 30:4, 38:4, 39:4, 44:4, 45:4, 46:4, 48:4, 57:4, 61:4, 65:4, 76:4, 77:4, 78:4, 100:4, 104:4, 107:4, 114:4, 133:4, 137:4, 142:4, 148:4, 157:4, 169:4, 171:4, 1:5, 4:5, 5:5, 8:5, 9:5, 14:5, 20:5, 24:5, 25:5, 27:5, 30:5, 31:5, 33:5, 34:5, 42:5, 45:5, 47:5, 54:5, 55:5, 56:5, 58:5, 64:5, 66:5, 68:5, 77:5, 81:5, 86:5, 88:5, 89:5, 93:5, 94:5, 95:5, 96:5, 97:5, 98:5, 99:5, 100:5, 108:5, 112:5, 118:5, 119:5, 123:5, 124:5, 126:5, 127:5, 129:5, 136:5, 1:6, 3:6, 5:6, 6:6, 16:6, 20:6, 22:6, 25:6, 31:6, 51:6, 56:6, 57:6, 60:6, 87:6, 98:6, 105:6, 106:6, 113:6, 116:6

journey
    a discussion of
        life's journey
            7–57:5

J. Reuben Clark
    44:1, 79:3, 21:4, 28:4

justice, justification
    discussion of
        6–17:2
    rewards those who are obedient to God's laws
        17:2

justified. *See* **justice, justification**

key(s)
    8:P, 23:P, 26:P, 2:1, 13:1, 18:1, 87:1, 101:1, 104:1, 28:2, 61:2, 22:3, 23:3, 24:3, 43:3, 44:3, 57:3, 60:3, 76:3, 83:3, 94:3, 95:3, 97:3, 98:3, 121:3, 122:3, 136:3, 141:3, 156:3,

157:3, 164:3, 176:3, 179:3, 181:3, 184:3, 190:3, 191:3, 192:3, 198:3, 9:4, 62:4, 66:4, 89:4, 106:4, 146:4, 153:4, 159:4, 164:4, 182:4, 26:5, 46:5, 47:5, 54:5, 64:5, 66:5, 87:5, 88:5, 108:5, 134:5, 22:6, 70:6, 94:6, 106:6, 108:6

King Benjamin
20:P, 19:1, 20:1, 21:1, 22:1, 23:1, 24:1, 25:1, 26:1, 8:2, 66:2, 7:3, 8:3, 9:3, 10:3, 11:3, 20:3, 51:3, 67:3, 152:3, 9:4, 35:4, 39:4, 78:4, 120:4, 121:4, 126:4, 127:4, 170:4, 36:5, 42:5, 59:5, 62:5, 63:5, 64:5, 66:5, 106:5, 108:5, 39:6, 46:6, 48:6, 76:6, 79:6, 106:6

king(s)
15:1, 16:1, 20:1, 21:1, 23:1, 25:1, 49:1, 85:2, 90:2, 92:2, 94:2, 95:2, 5:3, 7:3, 9:3, 10:3, 11:3, 29:3, 45:3, 111:3, 112:3, 113:3, 119:3, 139:3, 152:3, 198:3, 199:3, 20:4, 39:4, 76:4, 100:4, 108:4, 134:4, 8:5, 9:5, 39:5, 51:5, 54:5, 58:5, 60:5, 62:5, 63:5, 89:5, 1:6, 2:6, 16:6, 26:6, 46:6, 58:6

Korihor
50:1, 79:1, 127:4, 175:4, 47:6, 88:6

labor. *See also* work
35:P, 37:P, 38:P, 42:P, 20:1, 24:1, 27:1, 30:1, 42:1, 84:1, 39:2, 7:3, 19:3, 55:3, 146:3, 171:3, 17:4, 19:4, 39:4, 58:4, 62:4, 70:4, 71:4, 80:4, 82:4, 83:4, 84:4, 85:4, 86:4, 87:4, 88:4, 89:4, 90:4, 91:4, 92:4, 127:4, 135:4, 136:4, 140:4, 141:4, 151:4, 152:4, 156:4, 174:4, 176:4, 183:4, 185:4, 4:5, 26:5, 32:5, 33:5, 50:5, 92:5, 93:5, 95:5, 122:5, 137:5, 48:6, 59:6, 60:6, 65:6, 66:6, 71:6, 72:6, 100:6

lack. *See* poor

Laman
101:1, 20:5, 27:5

Lamb. *See also* **Christ, Jesus**; *See also* **Exemplar**; *See also* **Jehovah**; *See also* **Savior**
18:1, 172:4, 98:6

lawyers
86:1, 90:1, 119:4, 103:5, 37:6

Lehi
17:P, 27:P, 63:1, 64:1, 74:1, 94:1, 52:2, 58:2, 78:2, 195:3, 21:4, 42:4, 59:4, 3:5, 8:5, 9:5, 10:5, 17:5, 19:5, 21:5, 23:5, 26:5, 28:5, 31:5, 34:5, 41:5, 42:5, 51:5, 52:5, 58:5, 67:5, 73:5

lies
30:P, 9:1, 18:1, 22:1, 51:1, 63:1, 72:1, 19:2, 97:2, 9:3, 55:3, 60:3, 95:3, 97:3, 117:3, 139:3, 160:3, 181:3, 13:4, 41:4, 47:4, 65:4, 74:4, 137:4, 142:4, 156:4, 166:4, 7:5, 9:5, 19:5, 26:5, 87:5, 2:6, 60:6, 67:6, 101:6, 112:6

Lorenzo Snow
78:1, 6:4, 15:4, 17:4, 31:4, 47:4, 4:5, 94:5, 95:5, 100:5, 131:5, 136:5, 148:5

love. *See also* charity; *See also* heart
2:P, 7:P, 9:P, 10:P, 11:P, 12:P, 17:P, 20:P, 21:P, 22:P, 24:P, 27:P, 28:P, 34:P, 39:P, 43:P, 19:1, 22:1, 23:1, 24:1, 26:1, 29:1, 30:1, 33:1, 34:1, 42:1, 49:1, 64:1, 65:1, 70:1, 71:1, 76:1, 77:1, 79:1, 86:1, 87:1, 89:1, 91:1, 99:1, 3:2, 4:2, 5:2, 18:2, 19:2, 27:2, 38:2, 41:2, 44:2, 50:2, 54:2, 56:2, 57:2, 60:2, 61:2, 62:2, 66:2, 67:2, 69:2, 70:2,

Index & Concordance

72:2, 73:2, 74:2, 75:2, 76:2, 77:2, 78:2, 79:2, 80:2, 81:2, 82:2, 84:2, 86:2, 93:2, 95:2, 96:2, 97:2, 98:2, 99:2, 17:3, 30:3, 33:3, 44:3, 47:3, 48:3, 49:3, 50:3, 51:3, 52:3, 56:3, 57:3, 61:3, 68:3, 74:3, 75:3, 85:3, 86:3, 87:3, 90:3, 91:3, 92:3, 93:3, 95:3, 104:3, 108:3, 109:3, 111:3, 113:3, 114:3, 117:3, 118:3, 119:3, 122:3, 124:3, 125:3, 131:3, 132:3, 134:3, 138:3, 139:3, 140:3, 141:3, 142:3, 146:3, 147:3, 148:3, 153:3, 154:3, 155:3, 156:3, 157:3, 158:3, 159:3, 168:3, 169:3, 170:3, 171:3, 173:3, 178:3, 182:3, 185:3, 189:3, 203:3, 2:4, 19:4, 21:4, 23:4, 25:4, 26:4, 27:4, 33:4, 34:4, 35:4, 37:4, 38:4, 41:4, 42:4, 47:4, 50:4, 51:4, 52:4, 54:4, 55:4, 56:4, 57:4, 58:4, 60:4, 64:4, 70:4, 72:4, 73:4, 90:4, 91:4, 93:4, 95:4, 97:4, 98:4, 99:4, 100:4, 102:4, 107:4, 114:4, 116:4, 120:4, 121:4, 123:4, 138:4, 141:4, 142:4, 143:4, 146:4, 147:4, 148:4, 149:4, 152:4, 153:4, 155:4, 156:4, 157:4, 158:4, 163:4, 164:4, 165:4, 166:4, 167:4, 168:4, 169:4, 170:4, 171:4, 172:4, 173:4, 174:4, 175:4, 178:4, 179:4, 181:4, 182:4, 183:4, 184:4, 185:4, 186:4, 2:5, 16:5, 24:5, 30:5, 33:5, 42:5, 43:5, 52:5, 64:5, 66:5, 67:5, 69:5, 70:5, 71:5, 74:5, 77:5, 78:5, 79:5, 81:5, 85:5, 89:5, 92:5, 100:5, 106:5, 107:5, 108:5, 122:5, 124:5, 127:5, 133:5, 135:5, 137:5, 2:6, 5:6, 7:6, 8:6, 9:6, 11:6, 13:6, 15:6, 16:6, 18:6, 23:6, 31:6, 35:6, 38:6, 39:6, 43:6, 61:6, 66:6, 67:6, 70:6, 78:6, 79:6, 80:6, 85:6, 86:6, 87:6, 88:6, 91:6, 93:6, 94:6, 95:6, 96:6, 97:6, 98:6, 99:6, 100:6, 101:6, 102:6, 106:6, 107:6, 108:6, 113:6, 116:6, 117:6

low
> to make, is not demeaning
>> 34:4

Lucifer. *See also* **adversary**; *See also* **devil**; *See also* **hell**; *See also* **Satan**
> 10:1

lukewarm
> being, is a one-way ticket to hell
>> 47:1

Mahan
> 51:1, 52:1, 69:1, 79:1, 127:4, 151:4, 47:6

mammon. *See also* **materialism**; *See also* **money**; *See also* **riches**
> a discussion of
>> choosing, over God
>>> 99–137:4
> making friends with
>> 109:4

mansions
> 37:P, 76:1, 73:2, 82:2, 86:2, 89:2, 93:2, 168:3, 203:3, 81:4, 175:4, 50:5, 100:6

marriage. *See also* **new and everlasting covenant**
> a discussion of
>> how it's likened to new and everlasting covenant
>>> 72–99:2

martyrdom
> 34:1, 58:2

materialism. *See also* **mammon**
    25:P, 41:P, 62:1, 64:1, 68:1, 102:1, 109:4, 93:5, 26:6, 76:6

Matthew Cowley
    3:P, 4:P, 6:1, 46:1, 105:6

Melchizedek
    administered priesthood to Abraham/built temple in Salem
        16:1

Melchizedek Priesthood. *See also* **Aaronic Priesthood**; *See also* **oath and covenant of the priesthood**; *See also* **patriarchal order of the priesthood**; *See also* **priesthood**
    a discussion of
        4–209:3

merchandise. *See* **mammon**; *See* **money**

mercy. *See also* **grace**
    10:P, 17:P, 20:P, 21:P, 22:P, 23:P, 24:P, 23:1, 26:1, 30:1, 66:1, 100:1, 4:2, 6:2, 7:2, 8:2, 9:2, 10:2, 15:2, 16:2, 17:2, 18:2, 20:2, 23:2, 24:2, 26:2, 27:2, 28:2, 29:2, 30:2, 32:2, 34:2, 35:2, 36:2, 45:2, 57:2, 97:2, 54:3, 71:3, 156:3, 159:3, 165:3, 167:3, 98:4, 112:4, 122:4, 129:4, 130:4, 143:4, 148:4, 151:4, 179:4, 15:5, 16:5, 19:5, 44:5, 64:5, 77:5, 106:5, 113:5, 114:5, 124:5, 12:6, 29:6, 41:6, 49:6, 51:6, 82:6, 102:6

miracle
    17:P, 25:1, 30:1, 66:1, 64:2, 155:3, 9:4, 36:4, 51:4, 57:4, 60:4, 67:4, 70:4, 159:4, 160:4, 162:4, 163:4, 173:4, 25:5, 32:5, 39:5, 66:5, 101:5, 109:5, 99:6

miserable
    49:1, 50:1, 51:1, 60:1, 77:1, 78:1, 8:2, 16:2, 89:2, 132:3, 63:4, 13:5, 14:5, 16:5, 56:5, 30:6

money. *See also* **mammon**; *See also* **materialism**; *See also* **riches**
    love of, is root of all evil
        70:1

Moroni
    1:1, 31:1, 61:1, 90:1, 91:1, 92:1, 103:1, 12:3, 65:3, 68:3, 92:3, 166:3, 195:3, 209:3, 210:3, 5:4, 6:4, 107:4, 123:4, 124:4, 149:4, 165:4, 166:4, 174:4, 175:4, 178:4, 181:4, 182:4, 183:4, 31:5, 44:5, 53:5, 55:5, 70:5, 77:5, 109:5, 112:5, 118:5, 119:5, 22:6, 23:6, 43:6, 86:6, 100:6

mortality
    is testing ground for our genuine desires
        47:1

Moses
    4:P, 26:P, 18:1, 19:1, 28:1, 32:1, 34:1, 51:1, 74:1, 87:1, 88:1, 8:2, 22:2, 40:2, 81:2, 84:2, 14:3, 15:3, 16:3, 17:3, 18:3, 20:3, 23:3, 24:3, 40:3, 55:3, 63:3, 65:3, 66:3, 76:3, 77:3, 88:3, 89:3, 99:3, 104:3, 110:3, 175:3, 176:3, 177:3, 184:3, 195:3, 207:3, 208:3, 47:4, 50:4, 100:4, 101:4, 112:4, 118:4, 120:4, 126:4, 129:4, 151:4, 165:4, 166:4, 8:5, 9:5, 18:5, 23:5, 31:5, 32:5, 35:5, 41:5, 42:5, 54:5, 55:5, 67:5, 72:5, 74:5, 79:5, 86:5, 89:5, 112:5, 131:5, 16:6, 17:6, 29:6, 36:6, 38:6, 46:6, 49:6, 50:6, 94:6, 95:6

Index & Concordance 69

mother
: 46:1, 61:1, 62:1, 25:2, 51:2, 85:2, 59:3, 126:3, 158:3, 28:4, 110:4, 172:4, 21:5, 129:5, 27:6, 52:6, 98:6, 106:6, 109:6

murder
: 50:1, 53:1, 60:1, 62:1, 63:1, 69:1, 80:1, 90:1, 102:1, 96:2, 119:3, 146:3, 160:3, 53:4, 118:4, 137:4, 14:5, 108:5, 36:6, 60:6

murmur
: 22:2, 26:5

mysteries
: 26:P, 32:P, 39:P, 40:P, 18:1, 61:1, 44:2, 8:3, 10:3, 24:3, 30:3, 31:3, 43:3, 47:3, 49:3, 57:3, 72:3, 81:3, 87:3, 93:3, 95:3, 96:3, 97:3, 98:3, 176:3, 177:3, 181:3, 183:3, 187:3, 188:3, 189:3, 190:3, 191:3, 192:3, 46:4, 100:4, 108:4, 149:4, 59:5, 60:5, 66:5, 79:5, 85:5, 86:5, 87:5, 88:5, 116:5, 119:5, 16:6, 25:6, 115:6

natural man
: 25:P, 22:1, 78:1, 20:2, 21:2, 50:2, 178:3, 64:4, 95:4, 169:4, 182:4, 23:5, 25:5, 42:5, 43:5, 44:5, 45:5, 68:5, 76:5, 84:5, 91:5, 9:6, 86:6

Neal A. Maxwell
: 12:1, 40:1, 110:3, 118:3, 148:3, 15:4, 27:4, 57:4, 79:4, 148:5

needy. *See also* **poor**
: 3:1, 20:1, 24:1, 27:1, 56:1, 80:1, 91:1, 48:3, 114:3, 129:3, 7:4, 11:4, 14:4, 23:4, 24:4, 29:4, 33:4, 40:4, 54:4, 72:4, 75:4, 82:4, 90:4, 107:4, 117:4, 121:4, 122:4, 123:4, 124:4, 125:4, 126:4, 129:4, 130:4, 133:4, 139:4, 144:4, 149:4, 153:4, 158:4, 170:4, 179:4, 180:4, 71:5, 5:6, 8:6, 23:6, 36:6, 41:6, 43:6, 44:6, 45:6, 46:6, 50:6, 52:6, 56:6, 63:6, 67:6, 72:6, 76:6, 87:6, 95:6, 104:6, 105:6, 106:6, 107:6, 109:6, 113:6

Nehor
: 26:1, 84:1, 145:3

neighbor
: 7:P, 8:P, 9:P, 28:P, 30:P, 19:1, 29:1, 66:1, 18:3, 49:3, 96:3, 182:3, 21:4, 26:4, 33:4, 38:4, 56:4, 58:4, 77:4, 91:4, 100:4, 104:4, 118:4, 122:4, 158:4, 164:4, 165:4, 169:4, 184:4, 93:5, 94:5, 127:5, 16:6, 20:6, 36:6, 41:6, 77:6, 93:6, 94:6, 113:6

new and everlasting covenant. *See also* **marriage**
: a discussion of
    how it's likened to marriage
        72–99:2

Nimrod
: 51:1, 52:1, 53:1, 54:1, 55:1, 58:1, 61:1, 101:1

Noah
: 15:P, 14:1, 15:1, 16:1, 18:1, 36:1, 53:1, 55:1, 86:1, 87:1, 101:1, 102:1, 103:1, 7:3, 27:3, 207:3, 107:4, 32:5, 88:5, 101:5, 124:5, 125:5, 127:5, 22:6

oath and covenant of the priesthood. *See also* **priesthood**
: 1:P, 6:1, 32:1, 9:2, 34:2, 36:2, 47:2, 61:2, 98:2, 1:3, 2:3, 3:3, 4:3, 6:3, 21:3, 25:3, 30:3, 33:3, 35:3, 36:3, 39:3, 40:3, 41:3, 43:3, 47:3, 49:3, 53:3, 54:3, 55:3, 58:3, 59:3, 60:3, 61:3, 63:3,

64:3, 66:3, 68:3, 71:3, 72:3, 76:3, 77:3, 78:3, 80:3, 81:3, 82:3, 85:3, 87:3, 88:3, 90:3, 93:3, 94:3, 95:3, 97:3, 98:3, 102:3, 103:3, 104:3, 105:3, 106:3, 109:3, 115:3, 117:3, 126:3, 131:3, 135:3, 139:3, 140:3, 142:3, 143:3, 144:3, 159:3, 172:3, 173:3, 174:3, 175:3, 177:3, 179:3, 184:3, 189:3, 190:3, 193:3, 202:3, 208:3, 210:3, 211:3, 212:3, 213:3, 214:3, 1:4, 2:4, 14:4, 72:4, 90:4, 129:4, 142:4, 185:4, 1:5, 2:5, 59:5, 116:5, 134:5, 135:5, 136:5, 50:6

obedience
    30:P, 32:P, 41:P, 17:1, 19:1, 21:1, 48:1, 3:2, 4:2, 6:2, 7:2, 10:2, 12:2, 13:2, 15:2, 17:2, 28:2, 29:2, 33:2, 34:2, 35:2, 37:2, 38:2, 39:2, 42:2, 51:2, 61:2, 31:3, 67:3, 68:3, 71:3, 75:3, 80:3, 94:3, 118:3, 121:3, 124:3, 126:3, 131:3, 134:3, 135:3, 146:3, 203:3, 208:3, 212:3, 16:4, 18:4, 26:4, 36:4, 41:4, 45:4, 50:4, 56:4, 60:4, 65:4, 67:4, 102:4, 156:4, 180:4, 7:5, 33:5, 35:5, 36:5, 45:5, 46:5, 47:5, 81:5, 84:5, 97:5, 135:5, 18:6, 112:6, 113:6, 115:6

offence
    73:1

offering. *See* consecration; sacrifice; *See* offerings

offerings
    those, ordered by Satan are always rejected by God
        51:1

oneness. *See also* unity
    6:P, 18:P, 19:P, 12:1, 49:1, 92:1, 23:2, 24:2, 25:2, 27:2, 28:2, 29:2, 48:2, 71:2, 79:2, 170:3, 5:4, 18:4, 31:4, 41:4, 42:4, 43:4, 44:4, 45:4, 47:4, 59:4, 65:5, 94:5, 115:5, 123:5

opposition. *See also* adversity
    35:P, 33:1, 36:1, 54:1, 67:1, 70:1, 19:2, 26:2, 56:2, 117:3, 45:4, 62:4, 10:5, 18:5, 49:5

ordinance
    6:1, 11:1, 31:1, 51:1, 28:2, 31:2, 34:2, 36:2, 37:2, 38:2, 45:2, 53:2, 56:2, 63:2, 64:2, 67:2, 69:2, 91:2, 4:3, 6:3, 9:3, 10:3, 14:3, 16:3, 20:3, 21:3, 28:3, 29:3, 77:3, 82:3, 84:3, 87:3, 99:3, 105:3, 194:3, 197:3, 205:3, 212:3, 28:4, 43:4, 159:4, 160:4, 161:4, 162:4, 163:4, 25:5, 46:5, 60:5, 91:5, 133:5, 75:6

parent
    42:1, 46:1, 168:3, 53:4, 147:4, 153:4, 16:5, 62:5, 70:6

patience
    23:1, 27:1, 73:1, 22:2, 76:2, 85:2, 86:2, 29:3, 97:3, 129:3, 148:3, 149:3, 150:3, 151:3, 155:3, 178:3, 181:3, 99:4, 146:4, 155:4, 178:4, 184:4, 85:5, 15:6, 70:6, 101:6

patriarchal order of the priesthood. *See also* **Melchizedek Priesthood**; *See also* **oath and covenant of the priesthood**

Paul
    27:P, 39:P, 41:1, 57:1, 59:1, 70:1, 73:1, 88:1, 89:1, 91:1, 103:1, 27:2, 63:2, 64:2, 81:2, 85:2, 31:3, 40:3, 67:3, 90:3, 100:3, 149:3, 163:3, 171:3, 180:3, 189:3, 198:3, 37:4, 99:4, 117:4, 165:4, 166:4, 184:4, 13:5, 15:5, 29:5, 89:5, 119:5, 133:5, 15:6, 35:6, 76:6, 78:6, 94:6, 95:6, 97:6, 106:6

Paymaster
    8:P, 17:1, 151:3, 70:4, 71:4, 88:4, 90:4, 183:4

Index & Concordance

peace
: 2:P, 5:P, 8:P, 12:P, 17:P, 20:P, 26:P, 27:P, 9:1, 15:1, 16:1, 23:1, 25:1, 27:1, 30:1, 46:1, 88:1, 8:2, 24:2, 39:2, 50:2, 51:2, 61:2, 95:2, 5:3, 6:3, 7:3, 8:3, 18:3, 28:3, 29:3, 46:3, 50:3, 66:3, 70:3, 83:3, 114:3, 119:3, 129:3, 140:3, 167:3, 172:3, 173:3, 199:3, 19:4, 22:4, 40:4, 44:4, 46:4, 115:4, 118:4, 119:4, 124:4, 125:4, 137:4, 140:4, 150:4, 151:4, 152:4, 162:4, 171:4, 172:4, 178:4, 27:5, 28:5, 38:5, 44:5, 46:5, 53:5, 55:5, 81:5, 83:5, 92:5, 94:5, 103:5, 104:5, 106:5, 107:5, 122:5, 128:5, 130:5, 132:5, 133:5, 1:6, 2:6, 13:6, 34:6, 37:6, 38:6, 45:6, 60:6, 61:6, 64:6, 97:6, 98:6, 101:6

persecute
: 27:P, 28:P, 30:P, 61:1, 67:1, 85:1, 91:1, 137:3, 152:3, 108:4, 122:4, 123:4, 124:4, 150:4, 42:5, 26:6, 41:6, 42:6, 44:6, 77:6, 112:6, 113:6

plague
: 82:1, 160:3, 124:4, 38:5, 44:6

poor. *See also* **needy**
: a discussion of
    how we treat the,
        120–137:4

popular
: 14:1, 66:1, 81:1, 83:1, 84:1, 87:1, 25:3, 132:3

possession. *See* **mammon**

praise. *See* **popular**

pray, prayer
: 80:1, 85:1, 98:1, 14:2, 20:2, 55:2, 86:2, 91:2, 92:2, 41:3, 70:3, 154:3, 158:3, 192:3, 197:3, 8:4, 9:4, 45:4, 46:4, 54:4, 60:4, 111:4, 112:4, 140:4, 162:4, 163:4, 181:4, 4:5, 19:5, 42:5, 51:5, 53:5, 67:5, 69:5, 77:5, 78:5, 87:5, 112:5, 114:5, 115:5, 116:5, 120:5, 121:5, 122:5, 123:5, 124:5, 28:6, 29:6, 64:6, 90:6, 104:6

premortal existence
: mature knowledge of gospel from, planted deep in our souls
    44:1

pride
: neither rich nor poor exempt from
    24:1

priest
: 17:1, 26:1, 84:1, 20:2, 41:2, 94:2, 95:2, 5:3, 6:3, 7:3, 9:3, 29:3, 42:3, 46:3, 65:3, 119:3, 152:3, 190:3, 198:3, 199:3, 88:4, 100:4, 40:5, 63:5, 89:5, 16:6

priestcraft
: 26:1, 51:1, 53:1, 61:1, 68:1, 84:1, 85:1, 145:3, 146:3

priesthood. *See also* **Aaronic Priesthood**; *See also* **Melchizedek Priesthood**; *See also* **oath and covenant of the priesthood**; *See also* **patriarchal order of the priesthood**
: a discussion of
    Melchizedek
        4–11:3, 182–192:3, 204–210:3

oath and covenant of the
    39–60:3
restoration of the
    12–16:3

priesthood society
    1:P, 3:P, 4:P, 43:P, 3:1, 5:1, 6:1, 7:1, 12:1, 14:1, 46:1, 5:3, 6:3, 12:3, 21:3, 25:3, 28:3, 32:3, 35:3, 61:3, 85:3, 127:3, 206:3, 7:4, 14:4, 15:4, 22:4, 31:4, 74:4, 80:4, 90:5, 98:5, 99:5, 127:5, 87:6, 102:6, 105:6

princess. *See* **queen**

prison
    88:1, 51:2, 52:2, 54:2, 88:2, 70:3, 100:3, 138:4, 139:4, 151:4, 152:4, 12:5, 29:5, 39:5, 75:5, 63:6, 116:6, 117:6

probation. *See* **mortality**

progress
    perspective of our, compared to steps on an airplane
        90:5

properties. *See* **property**

property
    converting life into, is Satan's great secret
        47:6

prophecies
    93:1, 95:1, 97:1, 98:1, 109:3, 166:3, 4:5, 97:5, 103:5, 118:5, 119:5, 49:6

prosper. *See* **abundance**

publicans
    80:1

pure in heart. *See also* **Zion**
    2:P, 17:P, 25:P, 26:P, 38:P, 41:P, 43:P, 2:1, 3:1, 4:1, 6:1, 8:1, 12:1, 15:1, 19:1, 25:1, 33:1, 46:1, 48:1, 18:2, 47:3, 66:3, 71:3, 87:3, 161:3, 172:3, 178:3, 195:3, 207:3, 208:3, 2:4, 15:4, 16:4, 31:4, 73:4, 83:4, 95:4, 104:4, 109:4, 147:4, 1:5, 2:5, 3:5, 4:5, 18:5, 77:5, 78:5, 79:5, 80:5, 81:5, 82:5, 84:5, 87:5, 89:5, 90:5, 91:5, 93:5, 94:5, 95:5, 96:5, 101:5, 109:5, 114:5, 115:5, 116:5, 117:5, 118:5, 119:5, 120:5, 124:5, 125:5, 127:5, 130:5, 133:5, 134:5, 136:5, 9:6, 20:6, 26:6, 75:6, 76:6, 78:6, 116:6

purification
    14:P, 18:2, 19:2, 20:2, 90:2, 91:2, 66:3, 137:3, 52:4, 162:4, 182:4, 3:5, 25:5, 26:5, 75:5, 79:5, 90:5, 115:5, 116:5, 120:5

queen(s)
    93:1, 90:2, 93:2, 94:2, 199:3, 8:5

rainbow
    sign of everlasting covenant
        15:1

redeem, Redeemer, redemption
    noble spirits in premortal life carried out work of
        45:1

Index & Concordance

repent. *See also* **mammon**; *See also* **materialism**; *See also* **money**; *See also* **wealth**
    20:P, 2:1, 10:1, 13:1, 16:1, 24:1, 70:1, 91:1, 98:1, 99:1, 5:2, 7:2, 16:2, 17:2, 19:2, 35:2, 36:2, 96:2, 5:3, 6:3, 19:3, 45:3, 46:3, 70:3, 103:3, 135:3, 153:3, 161:3, 188:3, 205:3, 37:4, 69:4, 84:4, 102:4, 111:4, 112:4, 117:4, 118:4, 121:4, 126:4, 135:4, 136:4, 148:4, 15:5, 46:5, 78:5, 82:5, 105:5, 106:5, 109:5, 2:6, 18:6, 28:6, 29:6, 35:6, 36:6, 39:6, 46:6, 47:6, 59:6, 60:6

resurrected
    14:P, 13:1, 28:1, 64:1, 86:1, 95:1, 14:2, 26:2, 17:3, 91:3, 202:3, 203:3, 42:4, 13:5, 64:5, 105:5, 108:5, 121:5, 122:5, 132:5

revelation
    is key to magnifying callings and to learning
        95:3

riches
    30:P, 32:P, 34:P, 38:P, 17:1, 27:1, 31:1, 33:1, 67:1, 71:1, 72:1, 76:1, 84:1, 86:1, 92:1, 93:1, 95:1, 96:1, 97:1, 99:1, 123:3, 125:3, 126:3, 128:3, 129:3, 130:3, 131:3, 133:3, 141:3, 142:3, 146:3, 167:3, 171:3, 193:3, 8:4, 9:4, 10:4, 26:4, 30:4, 38:4, 40:4, 69:4, 72:4, 83:4, 84:4, 85:4, 87:4, 88:4, 91:4, 93:4, 95:4, 99:4, 100:4, 101:4, 102:4, 103:4, 106:4, 108:4, 109:4, 110:4, 111:4, 113:4, 115:4, 116:4, 117:4, 118:4, 119:4, 120:4, 123:4, 124:4, 126:4, 127:4, 130:4, 132:4, 133:4, 135:4, 140:4, 142:4, 144:4, 148:4, 149:4, 150:4, 152:4, 158:4, 184:4, 44:5, 103:5, 104:5, 4:6, 7:6, 16:6, 17:6, 18:6, 19:6, 22:6, 25:6, 26:6, 28:6, 31:6, 33:6, 34:6, 36:6, 37:6, 38:6, 43:6, 44:6, 46:6, 47:6, 48:6, 51:6, 56:6, 57:6, 58:6, 65:6, 67:6, 72:6, 113:6, 114:6, 115:6

Sabbath
    42:P, 37:1, 38:2, 39:2, 40:2, 50:2, 51:2, 72:2, 99:4, 53:5, 15:6

sacrament
    14:P, 23:P, 29:1, 14:2, 20:2, 36:2, 38:2, 39:2, 40:2, 41:2, 60:2, 67:2, 80:2, 81:2, 82:2, 89:2, 9:3, 11:3, 39:3, 42:3, 66:3, 75:3, 93:3, 165:3, 193:3, 210:3, 46:4, 17:5, 18:5, 60:5, 61:5, 62:5, 64:5, 117:5, 121:5

sacrifice. *See also* **consecration**; *See also* **offering**
    a discussion of
        3–31:4, 33–52:4, 61–92:4

Salem. *See also* **Jerusalem**
    3:P, 9:1, 15:1, 16:1, 5:3, 27:3, 29:3, 45:3, 1:6, 2:6

salvation, plan of
    50:1, 54:2, 25:3, 26:3, 31:3, 36:3, 68:3, 73:3, 12:5, 126:5, 130:5

sanctification
    14:P, 18:P, 18:2, 20:2, 21:2, 90:2, 91:2, 9:3, 56:3, 66:3, 67:3, 68:3, 69:3, 70:3, 71:3, 74:3, 75:3, 77:3, 84:3, 104:3, 137:3, 210:3, 14:4, 18:4, 21:4, 31:4, 52:4, 182:4, 3:5, 27:5, 47:5, 75:5, 79:5, 90:5, 94:5, 99:5, 115:5, 116:5

sanctified body. *See* **sanctification**
sanctuaries. *See* **mammon**

Satan. *See also* **adversary;** *See also* **devil;** *See also* **hell;** *See also* **Lucifer**
 we must understand, in order to confront him
  55:5

savior
 Adam empowered to become, to his family
  11:1

Savior. *See* **Christ, Jesus;** *See* **Exemplar;** *See* **Jehovah;** *See* **Lamb**

saviors on Mount Zion
 43:1, 32:2, 40:2, 25:3, 35:3, 37:3, 43:3, 66:3, 69:3, 104:3, 156:3, 144:4, 184:4, 64:5, 116:5, 68:6

science
 57:1, 81:1, 83:1, 14:2, 163:3

seal
 26:1, 24:2, 76:2, 79:2, 93:2, 13:3, 16:3, 17:3, 81:3, 84:3, 99:3, 149:3, 168:3, 194:3, 199:3, 209:3, 52:4, 75:4, 108:4, 155:4, 162:4, 38:5, 58:5, 65:5, 67:5, 25:6

secret combinations. *See also* **Gadianton robbers**
 49:1, 60:1, 61:1, 91:1, 97:1, 99:1, 102:5, 103:5, 108:5

selfish
 9:P, 38:P, 58:1, 73:1, 89:1, 91:1, 96:1, 19:2, 32:2, 71:2, 21:3, 74:3, 88:3, 122:3, 124:3, 125:3, 131:3, 137:3, 153:3, 154:3, 157:3, 171:3, 27:4, 55:4, 82:4, 91:4, 97:4, 98:4, 112:4, 117:4, 134:4, 140:4, 141:4, 145:4, 149:4, 152:4, 156:4, 165:4, 169:4, 176:4, 94:5, 11:6, 18:6, 29:6, 30:6, 31:6, 35:6, 37:6, 45:6, 48:6, 58:6, 64:6, 65:6, 66:6, 68:6, 71:6, 72:6, 77:6, 86:6, 88:6, 94:6, 108:6, 115:6

selfless. *See also* **charity**
 1:P, 8:P, 10:P, 12:P, 23:P, 25:P, 31:P, 24:1, 29:1, 5:2, 32:2, 71:2, 21:3, 51:3, 171:3, 109:4, 170:4, 93:5, 100:5, 26:6, 76:6, 87:6

Sermon on the Mount. *See also* **Beatitudes**
 14:P, 16:P, 28:1, 18:2, 82:5, 118:5

servant
 37:P, 16:1, 27:1, 34:2, 61:2, 62:2, 69:2, 87:2, 88:2, 91:2, 92:2, 96:2, 6:3, 30:3, 41:3, 72:3, 82:3, 100:3, 101:3, 103:3, 115:3, 196:3, 211:3, 214:3, 12:4, 49:4, 50:4, 53:4, 74:4, 75:4, 78:4, 79:4, 81:4, 89:4, 183:4, 66:5, 97:5, 110:5

set apart. *See* **consecration**

sex
 57:1, 66:1, 76:1, 154:3, 97:4, 11:6

single women
 64:3

slippery treasures
 110:4, 27:6

snare
 70:1, 73:1, 109:3, 122:3, 124:3, 139:3, 99:4, 103:4, 113:4, 14:5, 15:6, 19:6, 30:6, 108:6

Index & Concordance 75

Sodom
    1:1, 54:1, 55:1, 56:1, 57:1, 86:1, 94:1, 101:1, 102:1, 103:1, 5:4, 121:4, 23:5, 41:6

sorrow. *See also* **wailing**
    21:P, 34:1, 35:1, 63:1, 93:1, 102:1, 88:2, 51:3, 151:3, 160:3, 19:4, 124:4, 127:4, 136:4, 10:5, 43:5, 44:5, 106:5, 44:6, 48:6, 59:6, 79:6

soul
    11:P, 16:P, 17:P, 23:P, 43:P, 20:1, 21:1, 22:1, 28:1, 60:1, 76:1, 8:2, 19:2, 26:2, 40:2, 41:2, 49:2, 55:2, 59:2, 61:2, 94:2, 7:3, 19:3, 44:3, 47:3, 67:3, 69:3, 83:3, 97:3, 100:3, 102:3, 108:3, 116:3, 119:3, 122:3, 144:3, 151:3, 156:3, 159:3, 165:3, 166:3, 172:3, 175:3, 182:3, 184:3, 189:3, 193:3, 213:3, 2:4, 9:4, 16:4, 20:4, 50:4, 54:4, 56:4, 60:4, 64:4, 65:4, 111:4, 114:4, 115:4, 118:4, 127:4, 140:4, 146:4, 152:4, 155:4, 160:4, 162:4, 164:4, 166:4, 167:4, 171:4, 172:4, 174:4, 175:4, 179:4, 180:4, 182:4, 183:4, 186:4, 2:5, 13:5, 15:5, 17:5, 44:5, 45:5, 49:5, 68:5, 71:5, 74:5, 80:5, 81:5, 84:5, 100:5, 108:5, 122:5, 5:6, 6:6, 29:6, 30:6, 32:6, 33:6, 37:6, 48:6, 50:6, 65:6, 71:6, 85:6, 86:6, 91:6, 95:6, 96:6, 97:6, 98:6, 100:6, 101:6, 102:6, 103:6, 108:6

Spencer W. Kimball
    8:P, 25:P, 33:P, 3:1, 7:1, 37:1, 55:1, 85:1, 21:3, 31:3, 35:3, 118:3, 140:3, 191:3, 7:4, 9:4, 15:4, 17:4, 23:4, 30:4, 31:4, 48:4, 59:4, 83:4, 86:4, 109:4, 134:4, 172:4, 173:4, 177:4, 37:5, 49:5, 92:5, 93:5, 98:5, 100:5, 26:6, 57:6, 76:6, 88:6, 90:6, 98:6, 99:6

stewardship(s)
    in heaven based on stewardships on earth
        50:5

storehouse
    7:P, 36:P, 17:1, 18:1, 64:2, 6:3, 38:4, 39:4, 48:4, 61:4, 71:4, 72:4, 74:4, 75:4, 77:4, 79:4, 83:4, 88:4, 91:4, 96:4, 131:4, 10:6, 51:6, 77:6

submission
    79:1, 118:3, 152:3, 31:5

surplus
    36:P, 18:1, 48:3, 12:4, 24:4, 69:4, 74:4, 75:4, 79:4, 90:4, 91:4, 94:4, 147:4, 9:6, 114:6

telestial
    3:P, 9:P, 10:P, 12:P, 25:P, 26:P, 30:P, 31:P, 32:P, 37:P, 38:P, 3:1, 6:1, 7:1, 8:1, 10:1, 17:1, 29:1, 39:1, 40:1, 47:1, 66:1, 80:1, 103:1, 14:2, 15:2, 23:2, 48:2, 60:2, 68:2, 69:2, 68:3, 80:3, 89:3, 114:3, 117:3, 124:3, 125:3, 140:3, 141:3, 144:3, 164:3, 211:3, 10:4, 15:4, 18:4, 25:4, 34:4, 35:4, 36:4, 64:4, 69:4, 73:4, 82:4, 83:4, 96:4, 101:4, 105:4, 141:4, 147:4, 148:4, 163:4, 185:4, 11:5, 12:5, 19:5, 31:5, 36:5, 70:5, 76:5, 84:5, 85:5, 91:5, 121:5, 126:5, 10:6, 17:6, 21:6, 66:6, 86:6, 105:6, 106:6, 107:6, 110:6, 112:6, 115:6, 116:6

temple
    covenants, necessary to establish Zion/is gathering place for Zion people
        31:1

temptation
    70:1, 133:3, 176:3, 43:4, 97:4, 99:4, 14:5, 120:5, 121:5, 11:6, 15:6

Ten Commandments
    15:2, 100:4, 148:4, 110:5, 16:6

ten virgins
    85:1, 103:1, 87:2, 90:2, 92:2

terrestrial
    testimony, bearing of, purifies heart; bearing of, is an act of love
        56:3

tithes
    31:P, 34:P, 37:P, 42:P, 17:1, 37:1, 6:3, 8:4, 12:4, 13:4, 30:4, 81:4, 88:4, 89:4, 92:4, 96:4, 147:4, 118:5, 10:6, 12:6, 13:6, 51:6, 114:6, 115:6

tradition
    98:1, 72:2, 73:2, 75:2, 84:2, 7:3, 9:3

treasure. *See* **mammon**

trial(s). *See also* **adversity**; *See also* **opposition**
    29:P, 44:1, 56:2, 58:2, 83:3, 128:3, 148:3, 151:3, 124:4, 23:5, 27:5, 50:5, 58:5, 44:6, 50:6

unite, unity. *See also* **oneness**
    4:P, 6:P, 37:P, 3:1, 9:1, 14:1, 19:1, 68:1, 77:1, 78:1, 92:1, 23:2, 24:2, 25:2, 27:2, 69:2, 93:2, 74:3, 85:3, 114:3, 116:3, 140:3, 147:3, 170:3, 2:4, 19:4, 33:4, 41:4, 42:4, 43:4, 44:4, 45:4, 46:4, 47:4, 48:4, 49:4, 50:4, 51:4, 52:4, 54:4, 55:4, 58:4, 59:4, 60:4, 62:4, 82:4, 156:4, 171:4, 183:4, 185:4, 2:5, 50:5, 73:5, 100:5, 108:5, 97:6

universe
    composition of
        89:3

vain
    22:P, 28:P, 64:1, 66:1, 69:1, 80:1, 86:1, 97:1, 98:1, 41:2, 45:3, 47:3, 51:3, 92:3, 107:3, 110:3, 114:3, 119:3, 135:3, 146:3, 153:3, 163:3, 164:3, 99:4, 110:4, 111:4, 115:4, 117:4, 118:4, 119:4, 122:4, 124:4, 126:4, 127:4, 133:4, 149:4, 175:4, 181:4, 57:5, 71:5, 95:5, 101:5, 102:5, 104:5, 4:6, 15:6, 28:6, 33:6, 36:6, 38:6, 41:6, 42:6, 44:6, 46:6, 57:6, 79:6, 104:6

veil
    40:1, 55:1, 80:2, 83:2, 84:2, 85:2, 95:2, 26:3, 91:3, 102:3, 178:3, 179:3, 180:3, 181:3, 183:3, 196:3, 209:3, 210:3, 54:4, 12:5, 67:5, 68:5, 79:5, 85:5, 89:5, 109:5, 131:5

violence
    14:1, 36:1, 87:1, 93:1, 95:1, 8:3, 121:3, 108:4, 26:6

wailing. *See also* **sorrow**
    94:1

war
    17:P, 26:P, 42:1, 44:1, 55:1, 62:1, 69:1, 78:1, 80:1, 85:1, 91:1, 102:1, 28:2, 83:3, 108:4, 137:4, 37:5, 102:5, 103:5, 108:5, 26:6, 60:6

warn
    95:1, 113:4, 124:4, 102:5, 103:5, 30:6, 44:6

Index & Concordance

wealth. *See also* **mammon;** *See also* **poor;** *See also* **riches**
    a discussion of
        proper use
            120–151:4
        seeking
            99–137:4

weapon
    29:P, 57:1, 71:1, 55:2, 99:4, 109:4, 132:4, 149:4, 16:6, 26:6, 56:6, 112:6

whore. *See* **Babylon**

wickedness
    today's level of, equals or exceeds times that of Noah's generation
        87:1

widow
    93:1, 7:4, 29:4, 104:4, 109:4, 130:4, 140:4, 146:4, 153:4, 51:5, 70:5, 20:6, 27:6, 52:6, 65:6, 70:6

wife. *See also* **marriage**
    10:1, 33:1, 62:1, 24:2, 25:2, 58:2, 66:2, 74:2, 76:2, 77:2, 78:2, 79:2, 85:2, 92:2, 94:2, 95:2, 97:2, 13:3, 15:3, 17:3, 23:3, 31:3, 59:3, 82:3, 85:3, 110:3, 112:3, 126:3, 136:3, 183:3, 198:3, 199:3, 207:3, 211:3, 26:4, 41:4, 43:4, 45:4, 52:4, 98:4, 100:4, 156:4, 157:4, 10:5, 20:5, 24:5, 38:5, 42:5, 11:6, 16:6, 106:6, 109:6

wilderness. *See also* **Babylon**
    a discussion of
        our journey through the
            12–41:5

Wilford Woodruff
    40:1, 55:3, 131:3, 211:3, 148:5

wisdom
    21:P, 32:P, 23:1, 24:1, 26:1, 31:1, 33:1, 39:1, 59:1, 60:1, 64:1, 65:1, 78:1, 84:1, 98:1, 102:1, 45:2, 50:3, 54:3, 71:3, 93:3, 152:3, 161:3, 163:3, 164:3, 165:3, 166:3, 167:3, 168:3, 187:3, 201:3, 208:3, 6:4, 26:4, 27:4, 66:4, 77:4, 100:4, 105:4, 108:4, 109:4, 120:4, 122:4, 137:4, 141:4, 149:4, 152:4, 179:4, 65:5, 3:6, 16:6, 21:6, 25:6, 27:6, 38:6, 42:6, 61:6, 66:6, 82:6, 102:6, 115:6

work. *See also* **labor**
    Christ's, takes priority
        30:1

world, worldly. *See also* **Babylon**
    in, but not of
        74:1

yoke
    17:P, 23:P, 28:P, 62:1, 63:1, 101:1, 92:2, 160:3, 179:4, 68:5, 69:5, 71:5, 102:6

Zion
    an individual with a pure heart
        12:1
    begins in each person's heart
        1:1, 12:1, 13:1
    definition of, is perfection
        12:1
    is a return to the presence of God
        47:1
    is our ideal
        6:1
    principles of
        19:1
    we are
        46:1

Zion people
    characteristics of
        12:1
    temple gathering place for
        14:1

About the Author

Larry Barkdull is a longtime publisher and writer of books, music, art, and magazines. For nine years, he owned Sonos Music Resources and published the Tabernacle Choir Performance Library. He was also the owner and publisher of Keepsake Books. Over the past thirty years, he has published about six hundred products for numerous authors, composers, and artists. He founded two nonprofit organizations: The Latter-day Foundation for the Arts, Education, and Humanity (to promote LDS arts), and Gospel Ideals International (to promote the gospel of Jesus Christ on the Internet).

His books have sold in excess of 300,000 copies and have been translated into Japanese, Korean, Italian, and Hebrew. He is the recipient of the American Family Literary Award; the Benjamin Franklin Book Award; and *Foreword Magazine*'s GOLD Book of the Year Award for best fiction. His most recent books are *Priesthood Power—Blessing the Sick and the Afflicted; Rescuing Wayward Children;* and *The Shepherd Song.*

He and his wife, Elizabeth, have ten children and growing number of grandchildren. They live in Orem, Utah. Read more of his writings at Meridian Magazine.com.

www.ingramcontent.com/pod-product-compliance
Lightning Source LLC
LaVergne TN
LVHW081354060426
835510LV00013B/1823